PORTFOLIO

TRYST WITH PROSPERITY

Medha M. Kudaisya is a business historian. She is an associate professor at the department of history, National University of Singapore. She has published widely on India's business and economic history. Her publications include *The Life and Times of G.D. Birla*, *Chinese and Indian Business: Historical Antecedents* (co-edited with Ng Chin-keong) and *The Oxford India Anthology of Business History* (editor).

ADVANCE PRAISE FOR THE BOOK

'In this meticulously researched book Medha Kudaisya recreates the world of Indian business at its apex level in the 1940s. Drawing upon colonial records, newspapers and private papers of the key industrialists, *Tryst with Prosperity* brings alive the Bombay Plan of 1944. It argues with conviction that, as an economic blueprint for independent India, the Bombay Plan proposed a distinct path of capitalism with Indian characteristics, which would chart a middle path between state-led planning and private enterprise, enabling a creative partnership between the state and business'—Dwijendra Tripathi, eminent business historian

'*Tryst with Prosperity* is the first systematic study of the Bombay Plan, a remarkable initiative by Indian business to contribute to development. With a readable and commanding narrative, the book shows the economic, political and intellectual backdrop to the Plan, and shows why the story still matters'—Tirthankar Roy, professor of economic history, London School of Economics

THE STORY OF INDIAN BUSINESS

Arthashastra: The Science of Wealth by Thomas R. Trautmann

The World of the Tamil Merchant: Pioneers of International Trade by Kanakalatha Mukund

The Mouse Merchant: Money in Ancient India by Arshia Sattar

The East India Company: The World's Most Powerful Corporation by Tirthankar Roy

Caravans: Punjabi Khatri Merchants on the Silk Road by Scott C. Levi

Globalization before Its Time: The Gujarati Merchants from Kachchh by Chhaya Goswami (edited by Jaithirth Rao)

Three Merchants of Bombay: Business Pioneers of the Nineteenth Century by Lakshmi Subramanian

The Marwaris: From Jagat Seth to the Birlas by Thomas A. Timberg

Goras and Desis: Managing Agencies and the Making of Corporate India by Omkar Goswami

Indian Railways: Weaving of a National Tapestry by Bibek Debroy, Sanjay Chadha and Vidya Krishnamurthi

THE STORY OF INDIAN BUSINESS

TRYST
WITH
PROSPERITY

Indian Business and the
Bombay Plan of 1944

Medha M. Kudaisya

Introduction by
Gurcharan Das
Series Editor

PORTFOLIO
PENGUIN

An imprint of Penguin Random House

PORTFOLIO

USA | Canada | UK | Ireland | Australia
New Zealand | India | South Africa | China | Singapore

Portfolio is part of the Penguin Random House group of companies
whose addresses can be found at global.penguinrandomhouse.com

Published by Penguin Random House India Pvt. Ltd
4th Floor, Capital Tower 1, MG Road,
Gurugram 122 002, Haryana, India

Penguin
Random House
India

First published in Portfolio by Penguin Random House India 2018

Copyright © Medha M. Kudaisya 2018
Introduction copyright © Gurcharan Das 2018

ISBN 9780143445937

Typeset in Adobe Garamond Pro by Manipal Digital Systems, Manipal
Printed at Manipal Technologies Limited, India

www.penguin.co.in

MIX
Paper | Supporting
responsible forestry
FSC® C043100

This is a legitimate digitally printed version of the book and therefore might not
have certain extra finishing on the cover.

CONTENTS

CONTENTS

INTRODUCTION

*Planning and competition can be combined only by
planning for competition, not by planning against competition.
The planning against which all our criticism is directed is
solely the planning against competition.*

—F.A. Hayek

A tryst with prosperity or with tragedy?

Is Medha Kudaisya's account of the Bombay Plan a tryst
with prosperity or is it a tryst with tragedy? As a professional
historian, she has narrated the story with calm objectivity
and equanimity, driven only by data and research, leaving
the answer open to the reader. Her narrative begins with
optimism in the middle of World War II when a group
of highly competent, well-intentioned men with a proven
record of success, came together to plan the economic future
of India. It ends a decade later when the same men of high
ideals are bitter and pessimistic—they realize that their plan
has unwittingly produced the opposite of what they had

intended. In the process of creating conditions for wiping out poverty in India, they had planted the seeds for a 'command economy' and paved the way for what C. Rajagopalachari (Rajaji) called 'license, permit, inspector raj', thereby robbing the freedom of entrepreneurs and businessmen, the very persons who create jobs and wealth in a free society.

The ancient Greeks taught us that it is hard to blame anyone except fate when high tragedy strikes. So, I expect, is the case with the Bombay Plan and the subsequent ones that followed it in independent India. Neither the planners, nor Jawaharlal Nehru should be judged too harshly, for they were creatures of a socialist age—all victims 'of the zeitgeist, of the spirit of the times', as Ramachandra Guha puts it. Socialism was attractive to any sensitive person in those idealistic days. There was hope and the country was soon to become free. The class with money and influence was tiny and came entirely from the upper castes. It was natural for most Indians to expect that the government of free India should intervene on behalf of the masses; moreover, socialism had captured the imagination of the intelligentsia too. The leaders who had fought for decades for freedom were also in a hurry. They could not wait for the benefits to 'trickle down' through a market-oriented strategy.

If it is hard to blame Nehru or the authors of the Bombay Plan, it is certainly possible to fault Indira Gandhi, Nehru's daughter, who ruled India after 1970. By then, there was plenty of evidence from the rise of East Asia that there existed a better, more successful model of development. Unlike India's focus on heavy industry and import substitution, this model relied on the export of low-tech, labour-intensive manufactures. Despite being aware of it, Mrs Gandhi not only persisted with her father's wrong model but went further—she enacted more controls and tightened the Licence Raj. When individuals blunder, it is unfortunate and their families suffer. When rulers fail, it is a national tragedy.

What was the Bombay Plan?

'Bombay Plan' is the name commonly given to a set of proposals made by seven leading Indian industrialists and technocrats for the development of the post-independence economy of India. The industrialists were J.R.D. Tata, G.D. Birla, Sri Ram and Kasturbhai Lalbhai; the technocrats were A.D. Shroff, Ardeshir Dalal and John Matthai. Their plan laid out a comprehensive development agenda, arguing for rapid and self-reliant industrialization. They had a sensible goal of equitable growth and hoped to achieve it by doubling the per capita income in fifteen years—with half the investment going to industry, which was expected to grow fivefold while the agricultural output would double during this period. They assumed that the economy could not grow rapidly without government actively setting up heavy industry via deficit financing, creating thus a sizeable public sector. They also believed that the fledgling private industry of the country would not be able to compete in a free-market economy and argued for protection from foreign competition in the early stages.

Although the industrialists recognized the need for foreign capital and technology, they felt it had to be under state control. They preferred foreign debt to foreign direct investment, and wanted foreign ownership to be prohibited in essential areas such as banking, insurance, power and aviation. Where it existed, they wanted it nationalized. They acceded to a vast area of state control—in fixing prices, limiting dividends, controlling foreign trade and foreign exchange, in licensing production, in allocating capital goods and distributing consumer goods. More ominously, they were willing to accept 'important limitations on the freedom of private enterprise', and felt that 'rights attached to private property would naturally be circumscribed'.

The seeds for widespread state intervention in the nation's economic life were sown in 1938 when the Congress party set up a National Planning Committee (NPC), chaired by Jawaharlal Nehru, which outlined an economic policy for free India. It stated that 'national self-sufficiency' was the goal and the planning of 'consumption, production, investment, trade, and income distribution' were the means to achieve it. Although Nehru did not officially accept the Bombay Plan, his Fabian socialism loomed over it. He went on to become India's first prime minister and planning became a way of life under him. Kudaisya points out that subsequent official plans followed many of the principles of the Bombay Plan, which has given it almost a mythic stature among historians. Sixty years later, in 2004, the technocrat-turned-prime minister Manmohan Singh said the document was still relevant. He pointed out that the Plan had laid great emphasis on public investment in social and economic infrastructure in both rural and urban areas, and had stressed the importance of agrarian reforms and agricultural research, as also on setting up educational institutions and a modern financial system.

Optimism and pessimism

There were many reasons for optimism among the authors of the Bombay Plan. The author points out that the private sector was performing well in India, making enormous profits from producing supplies for the Allies during World War II. A spectacular transformation of India's debt position had occurred. Not only was India's sterling debt liquidated but the country accumulated a positive balance of 1.3 billion pounds by the end of the War. The planners saw this as an opportunity to make huge investments in plant, equipment and technical expertise from the West for an ambitious post-war industrial expansion.

Optimism pervaded the intellectual climate as well and these ideas would go on to become a new field of 'development economics'. Among its pioneers were Paul Rosenstein-Rodan and Ragnar Nurkse, who argued that poor countries required massive investment to overcome backwardness. Since businessmen did not have either the resources or the appetite for that kind of risk, it fell on the state to give a 'big push' to undo the inertia of a stagnant economy. The push would enlarge the market, increase productivity, and provide an incentive for the private sector to invest. As the market grew, economic growth would become self-generating and the poor country would eventually become rich.

There were also grounds for pessimism but they were ignored by the authors of the Bombay Plan. With the outbreak of World War II, the British Raj's involvement in running the Indian economy grew rapidly. Rationing, price controls and other bureaucratic interventions become necessary. While in other countries these controls were gradually dismantled, in India they provided politicians and bureaucrats with ready instruments to regulate the economy. Many of the controls that India groaned under for four decades—from 1950 to 1990—emerged from the Defence of India Act 1939 and its accompanying rules. Rule 81, for example, provided for 'regulating or prohibiting the production, treatment, keeping, storage, movement, transport, distribution, disposal, acquisition, use or consumption of articles or things of any description whatsoever'; and for 'controlling the prices (or rates) at which articles or things of any description whatsoever may be sold'. This rule allowed the government to set up 'controllers' who could control the prices and distribution of supplies and services. Rule 84 allowed the government 'to prohibit or restrict the import or export of all goods', and had other diktats too, such as regulating the access to foreign currency. The irony was that many of these controls imposed by the Raj had been lifted in Britain after the War but India chose to continue with many of them till 1991.

Planning versus market

The Bombay Planners assumed that the economy would be a 'partnership' between government and business, but that turned out to be a naïve supposition. They had been warned. Kudaisya points out in Chapter 4 that some of the authors of the Bombay Plan were familiar with the work of the Austrian Friedrich Hayek, professor at the London School of Economics, who had challenged Lord Keynes's ideology of an activist state. Keynes's thinking had become the reigning ideology of the times after it had successfully helped to pull the United States and other western democracies out of the Depression in the 1930s through deficit financing. Hayek, on the other hand, believed passionately in market outcomes and feared that national planning would lead to a command economy and 'the road to serfdom'. Instead of listening to Hayek's warning, the Bombay Planners cited the reassuring words of the Cambridge economist A.C. Pigou that freedom and planning were entirely compatible. In advocating a larger role for the state, they wrote that 'the distinction between capitalism and socialism has lost much of its significance from a practical standpoint . . . [and] there is now a large ground common to both'.

The issue of 'planning versus market' was intensely debated in the world in the 1930s and '40s. The debate began, curiously enough, among a bunch of Austrian economists. Those supporting planning—such as Oskar Lange and Abba Lerner—pointed to the failures of the market and its inability to ensure perfect competition. They argued that by planning and the use of computers, they could ensure that the right products were produced in the correct quantities and thus stimulate perfect competition. Their critics—such as Friedrich Hayek and Ludwig von Mises—retorted that the most powerful computers of the planners would never be able to acquire the billions of pieces of information on constantly changing consumer needs and preferences, and marry them to the resources of society, the production processes and the technologies. Even if they got the information, they would not be able react to it as speedily as the market. Moreover, in a planned economy, they argued, factory managers would not have the incentive to provide truthful and rapid information to the planners. Since they were evaluated based on how much they produced, they would try to corner excessive raw materials to ensure that they met production targets (to the detriment of other factories). Thus, the planned economy would have enormous waste and inefficiency compared to the market. Human self-interest in the market economy eliminated this inefficiency.

Over the centuries, human beings have dealt with the economic problem of survival either through custom or command or the market. Some communities organized society around custom, with the son following the occupation of his father from generation to generation, as in India's caste system. Others organized jobs by authority, with the pyramids of Egypt being built by the command of pharaohs. More recently, the Five-Year Plans of the Soviet Union were carried out by the command of the politburo.

A third system was the market. Historians tell us that the agricultural revolution happened around ten thousand years ago when for the first time there was a food surplus. Some farmers had more than what they needed and the sensible idea of exchange followed naturally. The first towns emerged as centres of exchange between 8000 BCE and 10,000 BCE. This became the 'market system', giving individuals the freedom to sell or buy, and the temptation of gain (not custom or authority) steered a person towards his occupation. In the interplay of self-interest, the tasks of society were carried out by an 'invisible hand', as Adam Smith put it. Since the hand is invisible, this system is difficult to grasp. It lacks the visibility of custom or command, and it is also difficult for the voter to see it at election time in a democracy. A politician finds it easier to win votes by promising 'visible' benefits such as free water and cheap power. This is why liberal reforms and deregulation are difficult to implement in a democracy.

But the authors of the Bombay Plan were businessmen and they should have known better. In any case, their plan attracted much attention and criticism in India when it came out. The Left condemned it for its capitalist bias and its lack of attention to agriculture. The followers of Mahatma Gandhi felt that it betrayed the great man's ideals of self-sufficient villages and ignored the ordinary man. Some businessmen criticized its wide-ranging acceptance of governmental control; they were frightened by the language of statements such as 'practically every aspect of economic life will have to be rigorously controlled by the Government'. The economists did not believe that the economy could generate the capital required, and criticized it for the inflationary impact of such a massive investment in a short period.

Why did private industrialists with visceral aversion to socialism make out a strong case for central planning? Was it well-meaning nationalism on their part and a genuine commitment to the public good? Or, perhaps, it was the trust that political leaders of that generation inspired in all Indians, having selflessly led the struggle for freedom. Like most Indians, they also believed that free trade and laissez-faire policies of the British Raj had led to the exploitation of their country by foreigners, and concluded that piecemeal growth based entirely on market forces might not bring about rapid development. Or was it self-seeking behaviour—the huge investment by the state would, after all, provide opportunities for profit to the private sector? When it came to protection, there was certainly self-interest involved—businessmen had gained enormously from the high tariffs on imported goods since the 1920s, and it was natural that they should want them to continue. Whatever the reasons, they dug their graves by proposing a domineering state.

The more politically tuned among the planners possibly felt reassured that despite the rising tide of socialism in the left wing of the Congress party, there were also many pro-business, right-of-centre leaders who had the seniority and gravitas to take on Nehru and the left wing. This list was headed by Mahatma Gandhi who was anything but a socialist, but there were other powerful and charismatic figures such as C. Rajagopalachari, Vallabhbhai Patel and Rajendra

Prasad. Alas, they could not have known that Gandhi would be assassinated six months after Independence; Patel would die in December 1950; Rajagopalachari would effectively exile himself from national politics; and Prasad would be elevated to the ceremonial, ineffectual position of the first President of the country. All this would leave the field open for Nehru and his socialist cronies.

In the end, the hope of rapid economic growth did not materialize. True, the economy grew better than in the colonial era. Compared to 1 per cent growth between 1900 and 1950, growth climbed to 6.2 per cent during Nehru's reign. But it quickly plummeted during Indira Gandhi's rule to levels even below other Third World countries. India averaged a growth rate of 3.5 per cent per year for three decades until 1980. Of this, 2.2 per cent was neutralized by a population growth of 2.5 per cent, leaving around 1 per cent in terms of per capita growth. This was what economists moaned about, calling it 'the Hindu rate', when of course, it had nothing to do with 'Hindu', but everything to do with the Licence Raj.

What went wrong?

What lessons can we draw from the Bombay Plan? It seems to me there were at least five major mistakes in the plan's mantra and they were compounded in 1956 by a new industrial policy resolution and the Second Five-Year Plan under P.C. Mahalanobis. One, it adopted an inward-looking, import-substituting path rather than an outward-looking, export-promoting route, thus denying the nation the prosperity that world trade brought for three decades after the end of World War II. Import substitution led local businessmen to reinvent the wheel, resulting in the manufacture of poor quality, high-cost goods without any reference to comparative advantage. Two, it suggested setting up a sizeable public sector, which, in practice, became monopolistic and inefficient, while also being denied autonomy in its functioning. Three, it opened the door for regulating private enterprise, which ended in creating a nightmare of controls; the licensing regime diminished competition, instead of encouraging it. Four, it discouraged foreign capital and denied the nation the benefits of new technology. Five, it ignored the education and health of the children.

The planners made the mistake of focusing on how to raise savings, naively assuming that once the government made the investments, the returns would come automatically. In reality, the state-owned monopolies turned out to be hopelessly inefficient. It would have made all the difference had the planners laid out the minimum acceptable targets of profitability, and planned for the training of managers in the public enterprises. At the root of the problem was the blunder in believing that the state could become an entrepreneur.

It never made sense to close an industry to the private sector—this was tantamount to discouraging enterprise. The successful countries of the Far East practised the opposite policy in the 1960s. In Korea, for example, the government offered cheap credit to private business when it did not have the resources necessary to set up strategic and basic industries. The Tatas made 119 proposals between 1960 and 1989 to start new business or expand old ones, and all of them ended in the wastebaskets of the bureaucrats. Aditya Birla, the young and dynamic inheritor of the Birla empire, who had trained at Massachusetts Institute of Technology, was so disillusioned with Indian policy that he decided to expand Birla enterprises outside India, and eventually set up dynamic companies in Thailand, Malaysia, Indonesia and the Philippines, away from the hostile atmosphere of his home.

What was most bizarre and damaging was a licensing system which began with the Industrial Licensing Act of 1951. The purpose of licensing was: (a) to create a planned pattern of investment; (b) to counteract monopoly and the concentration of wealth; (c) to maintain regional balance in locating industries; (d) to protect the interests of small-scale producers and encourage the entry of new entrepreneurs; and (e) to encourage optimum scale of plants and advanced technology. All these were good intentions but the way the bureaucracy went about administrating the system created terrifying red tape. An untrained bunch of low-level functionaries at the Directorate General of Technical Development, operating on the basis of inadequate and ill-organized information and lack of clear-cut criteria, vetted thousands of applications on an ad hoc basis. They took months in a futile micro-review of an application and finally sent it for approval to the administrative ministry.

The ministry again lost months reviewing the same data before it sent the application to an inter-ministerial licensing committee of senior bureaucrats, who were equally ignorant of entrepreneurial realities, and who also operated upon ad hoc criteria in the absence of well-ordered priorities. Once it cleared the licensing committee, it was sent to the minister for final approval. After the minister's approval, the investor had to seek sanction from the capital goods licensing committee for the import of machinery. If a foreign collaboration was involved, an inter-ministerial foreign agreements committee also had to give its consent. If finance was needed from a state financial institution, the same scrutiny had to be repeated afresh. The result was enormous delays, sometimes lasting years, thereby opening up varying opportunities for corruption. By the time the back-breaking process of moving files from office to office was completed, many an entrepreneur had lost the will to set up the enterprise.

Large business houses, on the other hand, set up parallel bureaucracies in Delhi, to follow up on their files, organize bribes and win licences. Since the system was based on first come, first served, the bigger houses realized that they could corner a considerable amount of targeted capacity by putting in multiple and early applications for the *same* product. Thus, they could 'foreclose capacity' without any intention of implementing the successful licence application. Some Birla trading companies pre-empted many licences in this manner. If the entrepreneur did finally get started and made a success of his enterprise, he was again in trouble. It was an offence punishable under the law to manufacture beyond the capacity granted by the licence. India became the only country in the world where the production of goods sorely needed by the people was punishable by law.

Tragically, the system ended up thwarting competition, entrepreneurship and growth, without achieving any of its social objectives. It fostered monopolies and led to the proliferation of uneconomic-scale plants in remote, uncompetitive locations, employing second-rate technology. The endless delay in clearing applications discouraged the entry of efficient and honest new entrants, and rewarded wily old, inefficient producers who could manipulate the system. In many cases, the basic entrepreneurial decisions on the choice of technology, the size and location of plants, which impacted costs and prices, were taken away from risk-taking businessmen and were made by bureaucrats who did not have a clue about the basics of running a business. Thus, licensing was an unmitigated disaster. It raised costs, brought delays, arbitrariness and corruption, and achieved nothing. We killed at birth any hope for an industrial revolution.

Finally, the failure of the Bombay Plan and of subsequent planning in India was due to the lack of state capacity. The problem of the mixed economy was of performance, not just of faith. Indians have learnt from painful experience that the state does not necessarily work on behalf of the people. It works often on behalf of itself—the politicians, bureaucrats, and the interests which directly support them. State employees in India went on to become a powerful vested interest, and they were not accountable. Although India relies more on markets now, it still needs clean and efficient regulators. The irony is that while the nation has been able to establish the more difficult political institutions of democracy, good governance continues to elude it. If the government had paid more attention early on to enhance state capacity and reformed the institutions of governance, even the Bombay Plan and subsequent plans could have been more successful.

What were the alternatives?

The Far East countries proved India's development model wrong. Beginning with Japan and followed by the four dragons—Korea, Taiwan, Hong Kong and Singapore—East Asia embarked on a strategy of penetrating the world markets through the export of low-cost manufactures, and they were rewarded by an enormous expansion in world trade in the 1950s and 1960s. They showed to the world that not only could they grow rapidly but they could also ameliorate poverty. The rest of the Third World, which mostly followed India's model, missed the bus. The development economists also turned out to be hopelessly optimistic about the poor countries' ability to transform their economies through investment in import-substituting manufactures, and overly pessimistic about their ability to export. They were aided by investments in education and health, which helped to create the initial conditions, both of growth and equity.

During the early years of planning in the 1950s, there was an alternative Indian vision articulated by two Bombay economists, C.N. Vakil and P.R. Brahmanand. Their strategy was exactly opposite to the official government plans, which were about huge Soviet-style, state-controlled, capital-intensive plants, employing few people, and delivering low returns over long gestation periods. Their starting point was that India lacked capital, but it had plenty of people. The thing to do was to put people into productive work at the lowest capital cost, and they suggested employing surplus labour to produce simple consumer products—clothes, toys, shoes, snacks, radios and bicycles. These low-capital, low-risk businesses would attract loads of entrepreneurs and they would yield quick output and rapid returns on investment. Labour would produce the goods that it would eventually consume with the wages that it earned from producing them. They were called 'wage-goods' because the wage earner would create the demand for the goods that he produced.

The 'wage-goods' strategy would have pushed investments in agriculture, rural infrastructure, agro industry and simple consumer manufactures for both home and export markets. It would have meant postponing the ambitious projects in capital and heavy industry. India would have imported the capital goods in the near term, and the foreign exchange for their import would have been earned from the export of simple consumer manufactures—the sort of products that Japan and the Asian Tigers started with. The result would have been high economic growth, high employment, rising exports and prosperity. It was a suitable strategy for a poor country like India. It is a great tragedy of history that no one paid attention to Vakil and Brahmanand's model, certainly no one in the government. The Indian intelligentsia was mesmerised by the apparent success of the USSR and wanted big steel plants.

India's planning betrayed two generations in the end. In stubbornly persisting with the wrong model of development, especially after 1970 when there was clear evidence that this path was doomed, growth got suppressed. It is sad that that most of the country's leaders at the time were men and women of goodwill and were widely admired; but when it came to the economy, they pig-headedly refused to change course, citing the name of the poor. The worst indictment of such planning is that it did very little for the poor. Only after the stranglehold of the Licence Raj was loosened did India's poor begin to climb out of poverty.

Ultimately, India paid a heavy price for its leaders' scepticism about the market's ability to allocate resources wisely. They did not trust profit to reflect economic efficiency. Neither did they think that Indian entrepreneurs had the will or the resources to make the investments needed to transform the country rapidly. They were under the spell of the Soviet economic miracle and this led to a bias towards heavy industry and against agriculture and light consumer industry. They assumed that India could not export and would always be short of foreign exchange. Therefore, they had to depend on substituting imported products, especially capital goods. These assumptions turned out to be wrong.

Legacy of planning

It is seventy years since the Bombay Plan was written. This period has witnessed the global collapse of communism in 1989 and the dismantling of India's Licence Raj beginning in 1991. Indians began their schooling in democracy in 1950 but they did not begin to enjoy economic freedom until forty years later. The fundamental premise of India's Five-Year Plans—to place the state at the 'commanding heights of the economy'—stands discredited. All Indian governments after 1991 have kept reforming, albeit slowly, but even slow reforms have added up to make India one of the world's fastest-growing economies. Prosperity is indeed spreading but it is happening amidst appalling governance. Indians despair over the delivery of the simplest public services. Where the state is desperately needed—to provide law and order, education, health and water—it performs poorly. Where it is not needed, it is still hyperactive, tying people in miles of red tape.

The problem of the lack of state capacity persists. State employees in India have become a powerful vested interest who are not accountable. Governance at all levels is woeful and confidence in government institutions remains low. Although India relies more on markets now, it still needs clean and efficient regulators. If the government had paid more attention earlier to enhance state capacity and reformed the institutions of governance, even the Bombay Plan would have been more successful.

Another legacy of forty years of socialism and planning is that the old mindset persists. Despite the market having generated widespread prosperity after 1991, people still distrust it, and capitalism has not yet found a comfortable home in India. Although people see the wondrous spectacle of thousands of young Indians starting new business ventures, the idea that their struggle for personal gain might actually promote the good of the whole society is too bizarre for most people. This may be because no one seems to be in charge in the market system. The consequence is that the nation continues to reform by stealth. No political party has dared to explain to the people the difference between being 'pro-market' and 'pro-business', leaving the impression that liberal reform mostly helps the rich. People do not understand that being pro-market is to believe in competition, which helps keep prices low, raises the quality of products, and leads to a 'rules based capitalism' that serves everyone. To be pro-business, on the other hand, means to allow politicians and officials to retain power over licences, which distorts the market's authority over economic decisions, and leads to 'crony capitalism'. This confusion partially explains the timidity of reform, and prevents India from performing to its potential.

Gurcharan Das

PREFACE

Tryst with Prosperity recounts the story of the 'Bombay Plan' (formally titled *A Brief Memorandum Outlining a Plan of Economic Development for India*) of 1944. A ninety-page document, published in two parts in January and December 1944, the Bombay Plan was authored by leading personages from the world of Indian business and commerce.[1] At a critical moment in the closing phase of British colonial rule, it outlined a bold economic blueprint for India's transformation with ambitious developmental targets for a post-War independent nation. The Bombay Plan embodied the idea of sharing new economic opportunities across different sections of society, together with a strategy for India's expeditious transformation. At the Plan's heart lay the promise of uplifting India from the cycle of grinding poverty and economic backwardness in which it had come to be mired after 200 years of colonial rule. The Plan advocated a capitalist path, yet a path customized to address India's gigantic developmental needs and problems. It had the audacious intent to consign forever to the dustbin of history glaring income inequalities, economic deprivation and lack of basic education and healthcare facilities.

In raising such hopes, the Bombay Plan captured the spirit of the era. India stood at the threshold of momentous change at the time of the Plan's publication. By 1942, wartime production had propelled India to the position of the eighth most industrialized country in the world. The Indian Army's deployment in Allied military campaigns overseas had brought about a stunning transformation in India's financial relationship with Britain, with India now emerging as a creditor with substantial sterling balances. Moreover, the closing years of the War raised expectations of an early end to colonial rule.

In such an atmosphere of hope and anticipation, nine individuals who wielded considerable influence in the commercial and business world—Purshottamdas Thakurdas, J.R.D. Tata, G.D. Birla, Kasturbhai Lalbhai, Lala Shri Ram, A.D. Shroff, John Matthai, Ardeshir Dalal and P.S. Lokanathan—came together to prepare an economic blueprint for a postcolonial independent nation. While preparing this document, they all took the view that a 'national government' was essential 'for safeguarding India's economic and financial interests'. They took upon themselves the challenge of formulating some sort of a plan for the post-War economy. They expressed optimism that the end of the War would usher in a new era for India, a harbinger of prosperity for all. The mood was upbeat, and the authors of the Bombay

Plan exuded great confidence regarding India's post-War future.[2] Holding out the promise of prosperity for all, the Bombay Plan promised to double India's per capita income within fifteen years, envisaging a 130 per cent rise in agricultural output, a 500 per cent increase in industry and a 200 per cent increase in services. Confident that a minimum standard of living could be achieved for the common man and 'gross inequalities in the incomes of different classes and individuals' obliterated, the Bombay Plan hoped that the existent 'pyramid of wealth and income' would be 'replaced by an even surface'.[3]

At a deeper level, the Bombay Plan represented a search for a new style of capitalism, 'a capitalism with Indian characteristics' that would chart a middle path between state-led planning and private enterprise, enabling a creative partnership between the state and market. The authors of the Bombay Plan wanted the Indian state to occupy the middle ground between laissez-faire and interventionist Keynesianism, with its actions and policies harmonized within the parameters of a developmental state. Planning was not seen as antithetical to, or incompatible with, a market economy. Rather, the architects of the Bombay Plan saw complete compatibility of planning with capitalism and envisaged a 'mixed' economy in which the state and the private sector would have complementary, even inter-changeable roles, thus proposing an almost visionary compromise between the two systems of free market operations and state control in independent India. The Bombay Planners unanimously advocated that centralized planning was imperative for achieving rapid economic growth, and encouraged a strong partnership between the nascent Indian nation state and private enterprise. The envisaged partnership was predicated on the premise that private enterprise would willingly join hands with the Indian state to chart a grand economic trajectory for the nation so that all sections of society would benefit from rapid development and share the prosperity that would follow. And, of course, the Bombay Plan's authors believed that as patriots and leaders of private enterprise, they themselves would play a critical role in bringing about this historic transformation.

The Bombay Plan envisioned the economic unity of India with a strong centre exercising its jurisdiction over monetary and fiscal matters through the length and breadth of the country. Within this framework, the Plan mandated a critical economic responsibility for the state which would, at least in the short term, take up a distributive role to ensure a minimum level of income for all citizens, and work towards minimizing glaring inequalities. Significantly, its authors believed a democratic political framework was a fundamental prerequisite for the Plan's successful execution. Although the state had to play an interventionist role, yet it had to be democratic. There could be no compromise with the 'belief that the freedom of the individual to give full expression to his personality is one of the supreme values of life and among its basic needs'. However, in the initial phase of 'intensive planning', there could be a temporary 'restriction of individual freedom', but this would be of 'limited duration and confined to specific purposes'.

Considering its groundbreaking ideas, its boldness of vision, its extraordinary timing and, not the least, the eminence and stature of its authors, the Bombay Plan was invested with exceptional significance. Seventy-five years after it was written, the Bombay Plan's legacy continues to be unmistakable in the economic life of contemporary India. Its imprint is manifest in the 'mixed economy' trajectory that modern India has adopted, and in the underlying philosophy, approach and structure of the national Five-Year Plans.

Yet, it is ironical that within a decade of its publication, the optimism generated by the Bombay Plan had begun to fade. The captains of business who had worked hard to prepare the Plan fell out with the Nehruvian political dispensation. Their ideas increasingly came to be ignored and they themselves sidelined. Why and how did all this come about? It is this story which this book hopes to narrate.

Tryst with Prosperity is organized around seven chapters. Each chapter reconstructs a specific dimension of the Bombay Plan. Chapter 1 describes the economic impact of World War II on colonial India. The War years marked the coming of age of Indian business and gave local business captains the buoyancy and confidence to

articulate their vision for post-War national reconstruction.
Chapter 2 outlines the spectacular transformation of
India's debt position which took place during the course
of the War. It also discusses how the sterling balance was
understood by the authors of the Bombay Plan, the lead
they took in raising this issue and the optimism India's
mounting sterling reserves engendered. Profiles of the
eight authors of the Plan (together with that of their
advisor, P.S. Lokanathan) are provided in Chapter 3. The
chapter looks at the authors' public engagements and
concerns, the intellectual influences upon them and their
relations with colonial officials as well as with nationalist
politicians until 1942 when the Plan was drafted. Chapter
4 attempts to reconstruct some of the key intellectual
debates that were raging then in international and national
economic circles and how they impacted the authors'
thinking. Chapter 5 analyses the operational aspects of
the Plan and its key aim of increasing industrialization
to ensure a 'decent standard of comfort' for the majority
without any radical redistribution of income. Chapter
6 tries to evaluate the public reception of the Plan and
the response of politicians (both British and Indian),
commercial bodies, economists, and, finally, its impact
on policymaking. Chapter 7 highlights the similarities
between the Bombay Plan and the Five-Year Plans,
including acceptance of the state's interventionist role in
the economy, co-existence of private- and public-sector
enterprises, the emphasis on heavy industry and the

reliance on deficit financing. Sadly, notwithstanding this valuable legacy of the Bombay Plan, its authors found themselves increasingly marginalized from the whole process of planning in independent India.

TIMELINE: 1938–1951

1938

The Indian National Congress constitutes the National Planning Committee, chaired by K.T. Shah. Members include Jawaharlal Nehru, Sir Visvesvaraya, Purshottamdas Thakurdas, A.D. Shroff, Ambalal Sarabhai, K.T. Shah and Meghnad Saha.

1939

1 September: World War II begins

3 September: Britain declares India a party to the War

27 October: Congress ministries resign in protest against the British declaration of India as a belligerent in World War II without consulting the Indian people

1940

15 October: Gandhi launches Individual Satyagraha with Vinoba Bhave as the first satyagrahi

1941

7 December: Japan enters World War II with attack on the US naval base at Pearl Harbor

December: Japanese invasion of Burma

1942

15 February: Fall of Singapore

8 August: Gandhi launches 'Quit India' movement

November: William Beveridge publishes *The Social Insurance and Allied Services Report* (*Beveridge Report*)

11 December: First meeting of the Committee on Post-War Economic Development (Bombay Plan authors) is held at the Tata headquarters, Bombay House, Bombay, to discuss the writing of the Bombay Plan.

1943

February: Ardeshir Dalal publishes *An Alternative to Pakistan*

Bengal famine

1944

17 January: Sir Purshottamdas Thakurdas, Tata, J. R.D Tata, G.D. Birla, Sir Ardeshir Dalal, Sir Shri Ram, Kasturbhai Lalbhai, A.D. Shroff and John Matthai publish *A Brief Memorandum Outlining a Plan of Economic Development for India*, Part I

March: B.N. Banerjee, G.D. Parikh and V.M. Tarkunde, as editors, publish *People's Plan for Economic Development of India*

June: Ardeshir Dalal is appointed as member of viceroy's executive council in charge of planning

1–22 July: United Nations' Monetary and Financial Conference held at Bretton Woods, New Hampshire, USA (also called the Bretton Woods Conference)

17 December: Sir Purshottamdas Thakurdas, J.R.D Tata, G.D Birla, Sir Shri Ram, Kasturbhai Lalbhai, A.D. Shroff and John Matthai publish *A Brief Memorandum Outlining a Plan of Economic Development for India, Distribution—Role of the State* Part II

1945

M.R. Masani publishes *Picture of a Plan*

May–August: Industrialists' delegation visit the UK and the USA (it includes J.R.D. Tata, G.D. Birla and A.D. Shroff)

Statement of Industrial Policy (Government of India) is issued

2 September: World War II ends

1946

October–November: Communal riots in Bengal's Noakhali district

1947

15 August: India gains independence

1948

30 January: Mahatma Gandhi is shot dead by Nathuram Godse (a former member of the Rashtriya Swayamsevak

xxxviii   TIMELINE: 1938-1951

Sangh) before the evening prayer meeting at Birla House, New Delhi

29 November: Constituent Assembly adopts a draft constitution

1950

15 March: Planning Commission is formed

15 December: Vallabhbhai Patel, the deputy prime minister, dies at Birla House, Bombay

1951

First Five-year Plan is launched by the Government of India (1951–56)

Industrial (Development and Regulation) Act is implemented

INDIAN BUSINESS COMES OF AGE: THE WORLD WAR II YEARS

War, production and profits

A 'godsend'; 'full of potentialities'; 'an industrial renaissance'.[1] In almost hyperbolic terms, Indian businessmen welcomed World War II (1 September 1939–2 September 1945) and the opportunities the war economy presented for 'furthering industrial expansion' in the country. Such sentiments resounded across local business groups and lobbies. The unique alignment of the needs of a war-fraught British empire and Indian expectations led to an outpouring of support for the British war effort.

The foremost business organization in the country, the Federation of Indian Chambers of Commerce and Industry—FICCI—avowed its whole-hearted support for the war effort when it met at its annual session seven months into the War in early 1940 (established in 1927, FICCI's membership included more than seventy-five major industrial, financial and mercantile associations). Acknowledging the 'strong and direct stimulus to the development of industries' due to the War, the FICCI president, C.S. Ratnasabapathi Mudaliar, asserted: 'What suits the war ought to suit the peace as well and nothing less than an effort to set India on her feet as a powerful self-sufficient industrial unit would be regarded as satisfactory.'[2] Session resolutions called upon the government to 'protect industries which are found vital in themselves', to 'undertake immediately *ad hoc* enquiries for granting protection to minor industries', to 'preserve India's exports and find new ones in place of those lost in the enemy territory', and to 'secure a fair share of the additional demand created by the war' for Indian industry.[3]

Without doubt, the War gave an immediate impetus to economic activity in India, with several opportunities opening up for import substitution. The real surge in production, however, came only after the first nine months of the War, with the fall of France, the entry of Italy and the spread of conflict to the Mediterranean. India now emerged as a supply base for all kinds of goods—an estimated 60,000 items were needed—for the Allied Powers on the eastern front.[4] Orders poured in from eleven countries of the British empire for a range of items, some never manufactured before in India. Amongst these were rail fish-plates, rail sleepers, acids and chemicals, and ammunition of all types, not to speak of more mundane items like khaki shirting.[5] The more established sectors benefited enormously, especially those directly connected with war needs, such as steel, coal, cement and textiles. A 'new India arises', proclaimed the *Times of India*, adding: 'A year of war has changed the economic face of India. Essentially an agricultural country though she is, her exports of manufactured goods have relegated shipments of raw materials to the background . . . We witness the spectacular rise of new industries, heralding the birth of an industrial India.'[6]

Official support helped ramp up production to record levels. This support took the form of provision of capital assistance for building factories; help in securing raw materials and stores, promulgation of the Defence of India Rule banning strikes; and relaxation of provisions of the Industrial Disputes Act, including the requirement that employers give notice before altering the character of production and, thereby, working conditions.

More diversified and on a stronger footing than it had been during World War I, Indian industry could rise quickly to meet the demands occasioned by World War II. Of course, there were disruptions, especially during the 'Quit India' movement (launched in August 1942), when widespread strikes and lockouts interrupted production. Sporadic communal disturbances also unsettled production. The Excess Profits Tax and Compulsory Deposit Scheme introduced in 1940 were other drawbacks, but these were minor irritants compared with the support industry received during these years.[7]

Not surprisingly, prominent business leaders rallied in support of the colonial state. They helped organize war-fund drives, much as they had done during World War I. In Bombay, the lead was taken by the veteran 'King Cotton' Purshottamdas Thakurdas, the young Tata Group chairman, Jehangir Ratanji Dadabhoy Tata (JRD), and Tata director and financial wizard A.D. Shroff—all three of whom were among the eight signatories to '*A Brief Memorandum Outlining a Plan of Economic Development for India*', or the Bombay Plan, as it was commonly known, published some months later in 1944. A Bombay Defence Loans Committee was set up, with JRD as chairperson and Thakurdas, Shroff and G.D. Birla's Bombay-based brother, Rameshwardas, as members. One of the most successful drives to raise money for the war effort was organized by JRD in the Tata company town, Jamshedpur, for the purchase of Spitfires, the famous single-seat fighter aircraft, and other fighter planes. In recognition, the Spitfires were named the 'Jamshedpur-Golmuri Spitfires' and the fighter planes 'The Singbhum War Planes'.[8] A pleased viceroy commended the Tatas in December 1941: 'Your investments in war funds have exceeded Rs 50,00,000 and your publicity committee has been doing most valuable work.'[9]

Perhaps even more valuable from the British point of view were the impressive quality and range of the strategic war materials produced by the Tatas. The largest producer of steel in the Empire, the Tata Iron and Steel Company (TISCO) had, by the end of 1941, shipped out about a million tonnes and, by the time hostilities ceased, had, according to JRD, 'provided approximately 3 million tonnes of steel' to the war effort.[10] TISCO's Control and Research Laboratories, set up in 1937, considered the finest in the Empire, were hard at work to produce almost 112 specifications of special steel which the war effort called for: steel for helmets, stainless steel for surgical instruments, tinplate and barbed wire, special alloy steel for machine tools, bullet-proof armour plates, and special electric cables (used for demagnetizing merchant ships). The production of the famous armoured car Tatanagar, which was fitted with bullet-proof armour plates and rivets, started in 1942 and soon came to be considered 'safer than slit-trenches during bomber raids'.[11] The viceroy, when he visited the Tata factory in December 1941, declared:

> The soldier who looks to you for your powerful co-operation will not ask in vain. He stands in the front line of battle, but you are standing at his shoulder, and it is the strength you give which will drive his sword-arm forward, carrying destruction to the Nazi and to all our enemies . . .[12]

Although by now the Tatas were best known for steel, they had actually started off in textiles with the Empress Mill in Nagpur in 1877 and still had a presence in the sector with four mills. Here too, demand boomed because of the War. This was a welcome turn in the fortunes of the sector that had been battling overproduction and falling exports through the 1930s. Now, with the onset of the War, 'depression gave way to sentimental optimism'.[13] Demand was phenomenal, especially for khaki uniforms, canvas and tents. In 1939–40 alone, the army bought an estimated 300 million yards of cloth. By 1942–43, this had quadrupled to 1200 million yards. Soaring production, especially of coarse and medium varieties of cotton, went hand in hand with rocketing profits. In 1941, profits of cotton mills were five and a half times as high as during 1938 and double that of 1940.[14] Taking advantage of the situation of rising prices, many mill owners engaged in speculative hoarding to make quick profits, and the government was eventually forced to intervene with the Cotton and Yarn Control Order of 1943. An official chronicler of the cotton mill industry conceded it was 'hard to deny that the actions of large sections of the industry were anti-social in character, even if they were not positively illegal'.[15]

Industrialists like Thakurdas, JRD, textile magnate Kasturbhai Lalbhai, the Delhi-based Lala Shri Ram and Birla (the latter three were among the other signatories to the Bombay Plan) benefited handsomely during these years. Kasturbhai did especially well because five of his seven textile mills produced coarse varieties of cloth, and most of his machinery and processing facilities were new, having been upgraded in the 1930s.[16] In the north, the War turned Shri Ram's Delhi Cloth Mills (DCM) into a household name. Its three factories quickly switched to round-the-clock production, making tents and ready-made garments.[17]

Like cotton textiles, another sector which had suffered during the global depression in the 1930s but now saw a huge spurt in demand due to the War was coal (for transportation needs). However, its production was held back after 1941–42 due to labour shortages. Cement too was in great demand during the war years—especially after the entry of Japan into the War—for the construction of aerodromes and other defence-related buildings.

The list of industries which experienced dramatic growth due to the War included sugar and jute. After the fall of Java and the Philippines in early 1942, Indian mills became the chief supplier of sugar for the British empire, besides catering to internal demand. Birla and his family had large interests in sugar, with five large mills. Shri Ram also had an interest in this sector, with Daurala Sugar Works, and began exporting in 1941.[18] Even a sunset industry like jute saw its fortunes improve because of the War. As early as in 1940, demand for jute in the first year of hostilities outstripped that of the period of World War I. Reflecting this rising demand, the average dividend paid by jute mills jumped from 6 per cent in 1938 to 10 per cent in 1939 and to 19 per cent in 1940.[19]

Besides these established sectors that saw a surge in war-related production, fledgling sectors such as machine tools (the number of engineering workshops increased from a pre-war number of 600 to 1500 by 1943) and chemicals (chemical plants increased from six to twenty-nine) too got a huge fillip.[20] For instance, Shri Ram added a chemical unit to DCM to produce acids required for dyeing, bleaching and other stages in the textile production process. The Tatas too were encouraged to enter chemicals and, with the support of Maharaja Gaekwad of Baroda, set up Tata Chemicals near Port Okha at Kathiawar in the state of Gujarat; the plan was to first manufacture soda ash, caustic soda and bleaching powder and then move on to fertilizers like potash and ammonium sulphate.

Phenomenal growth was witnessed in the armaments and subsidiary industries, to which state support was extended based on the recommendations of the Roger Mission (it arrived in India in late 1940 to advise the Indian government on ways and means of expanding industrial capacity for war production and was headed by Sir Alexander Roger from the British ministry of supply) and the Eastern Group Supply Conference (this was convened by the viceroy in October 1941 to coordinate arrangements for production and supply of munitions and setting up stores in various countries in South and East Africa, Asia and the South Pacific area.)

As soon as the War broke out, ordnance factories, railway workshops and civil firms were put to work in double, even treble shifts. Within the first ten months of the War, India had supplied 75 million rounds of small arms ammunition, 200,000 shells of all categories and 6000 rifles to commands in Singapore, Hong Kong, Egypt and the Middle East.[21] In the next two months, another 45 million rounds of small arms ammunition and 200,000 shells had been produced.[22] By March 1941, the large ordnance factories were backed by 250 smaller private workshops and twenty-three railway workshops; together, they produced 700 different items of munitions supply.[23] Ingeniously, even many plants not remotely connected to munitions, such as bicycle and motorcycle factories, started producing armaments.[24] By the end of the War, it was estimated that rifle production was ten times the pre-war output, 'light machine guns twelve times, bayonets seventeen times, small arms ammunition four times, gun ammunition twenty-seven times and guns and carriages nine times'.[25]

Military needs supported all kinds of industry. Soldiers needed shoes and combat boots, and demand surged from 100,000 pairs before the War to 6.6 million pairs by 1943.[26] Leather was needed not just for boots but also for harnesses and saddlery, and its production in 1942–43 was seven times that of 1940–41, with three-fourths of the production going to the army.[27] The military's need for soap and oil led the Tatas to set up a second oil plant in Bombay in 1939. War-time bestsellers included the famous Hamam soap launched just a few years before in 1931, 501 washing soap and the detergent Saf Karo. Other beneficiaries of the war economy included tailors (who stitched an estimated 120 million army uniforms and other garments in 1942–43, up from 40 million garments in 1940–41);[28] manufacturers of glycerine (used both for pharmaceuticals and for explosives);[29] and makers of cutlery and crockery (army kitchens needed a constant supply of both).

War dictated sentiments in the stock markets too. Share prices went through dramatic ups and downs, moving in tandem with Allied war fortunes. Although the capital market had begun booming in the mid-1930s, even before the outbreak of the War, because of the post-Depression global industrial recovery and low interest rates, the War catalysed a frenzy that continued through its duration. By the early 1940s, stock exchanges—and the number of securities traded on them—had proliferated across the subcontinent, with almost all large towns boasting of a stock exchange.

In the first few months of hostilities (till May 1940), the commodity and stock markets were dominated by speculation based on the fear that the War would lead to soaring prices in an economy not geared to meet its demands. Early news of German victory and imposition of the Excess Profits Tax led to a downturn from May 1940, but confidence began returning through 1941. The recovery in sentiment lasted till December 1941, when the Japanese entry into hostilities brought panic. By late 1942, however, as Allied successes picked up and victory became more certain, the Indian stock market began booming again, and the last three years of the War saw a frenzied rise in share prices.[30] The frenzy proved unstoppable, despite the introduction of Capital Issues Control in May 1943.[31] Optimism was such that, despite the introduction of Capital Issues Control, no less than 687 applications for either starting or expanding industries, involving an aggregate capital of Rs 25 crore, were received till the end of 1943. The 500 applications approved included permission for sixty-eight cotton textile units, fifty-seven iron and steel and engineering works, and sixty-three chemicals, dye and medicine factories.[32] In addition, the paid-up capital of joint stock companies, which is money received from shareholders in exchange of stock, rose from Rs 290 crore in 1939–40 to Rs 424 crore in 1945–46.[33] The glut of money and the difficulties inherent in starting new industrial enterprises led to a boom in the flotation of banks and insurance companies. The number of banks increased from 1277 in 1939 to 1600 by 1943, many with an unsound capital structure.[34] Business leaders became increasingly concerned that there could be a repeat of the post-World War I situation when over eighty banks which started operations during the war years went into liquidation.[35]

'Structural' changes in trade

Not just industry, trade too thrived. Positive news came on three counts: a marked increase in exports (the balance of trade in India's favour increased from Rs 9.4 crore in the year preceding the War to Rs 91.9 crore by 1942–43— *see table below*);[36] a change in the composition of India's trade, with higher exports of manufactured goods than of raw materials; and the opening of new markets like the US, which meant lesser dependence on markets within the Empire.

Trade followed the War's trajectory; official data show a quick rise in exports in the first year of the War, followed by a year of decline with the loss of European markets and transport and shipping shortages, then a substantial recovery from 1941–42 onwards, though there was a slight decline with the cessation of trade with Burma and the closing of the Pacific routes to America.[37] Overall, exports went up from Rs 172.4 crore in 1938–39 to Rs 198.8 crore in 1942–43. Simultaneously, imports dropped from Rs 163 crore to Rs 106.9 crore during the same period.

India's War-time Trade, September to August (Rs crore)

	1938–39	1939–40	1940–41	1941–42	1942–43
Exports	172.4	212.9	187.	242.4	198.8
Imports	163.0	161.4	175.2	134.5	106.9
	9.4	51.5	12.2	107.9	91.9

(Source: L.C. Jain, *Indian Economy during the War*, p. 55)

What was especially heartening was the shift in the composition of India's trade. In exports there was a remarkable increase in manufactured articles. Within the first year of the conflict, exports of manufactured goods had almost doubled in value; there was some decline in the second year, but the position improved in the following years. The overall value of exports of manufactured articles increased from Rs 476 million (Rs 47.6 crore) in 1938–39 to Rs 812 million (Rs 81.2 crore) by 1940–41.[38] Exports of foodstuffs too increased, especially of tea, grain, pulses and flour, but exports of raw materials fell, especially after German victories.[39] On the imports side too, even though raw materials continued to be a major component (54 per cent of total imports in 1943–44), the overall trend reflected a rise in imports of manufactured goods and a decline in imports of raw materials[40] (mineral oil was the largest single raw material import).

Another important change was the diversification of markets; trade with Europe almost ground to a halt while it greatly increased with non-empire markets, especially the US and the Middle East. These alternative markets quickly compensated for the loss of the traditional European markets. By mid-1941, approximately 50 per cent of India's exports went to the US and 17 per cent to South America.[41]

The US became an increasingly important trade partner. By 1942, exports to the US had reached $105 million, doubling in value from 1939, and constituted items such as jute, mica, shellac, manganese and chromite. American imports to India soared even more: valued at $378 million in 1942, they were nearly nine times more than in 1939. True, of this, $287 million represented lend-lease shipments, and commercial imports were only $91 million; but the value of commercial imports from the US was still more than double the pre-war figure in 1939. Not surprisingly, American industrialists were becoming attracted to post-war possibilities of trade with India.[42]

Overall, World War II gave a tremendous fillip to trade. Despite the loss of old markets, new markets replaced them and Indian exports increased more than imports. The economist P.S. Lokanathan saw in this a 'structural change' in trade and felt confident that India 'need no longer submit to a violent alteration of the terms of trade to her disadvantage'.[43]

Business and the Raj: expectations and disappointments

The outbreak of World War II had seen prominent Indian business leaders rallying in support of the colonial state. For instance, Thakurdas, at a town hall meeting in Bombay on 10 June 1940, promised to associate himself 'without reserve and wholeheartedly' with the war effort. Simultaneously, however, he had taken the opportunity to remind the colonial masters that 'whilst they (Indians) have been pleading, agitating and even resorting to non-cooperation during the last ten years to be allowed to be a self-respecting unit in the British Empire, a continually deaf ear has been turned to them'.[44]

Now, given their support for the British war effort, business leaders wanted to profit not only from an increase in temporary war-related industrial production; they were also interested in capitalizing on the long-term economic opportunities presented by the War, which they hoped would result in the development of basic industry in the country. As FICCI's president put it, the war effort meant 'not a mere transference . . . to Indian shores but a re-organization of Indian industry with a view to get the maximum output on the background of the full utilization of Indian resources'.[45] But the two sides had sharply differing perceptions about industrial development. Indian business leaders expected that the British would help develop basic industry in India, while the government was solely interested in producing goods for the War.

Such a dissonance in views led to early souring of relations between big business and government. The first issue on which differences surfaced was on the levy of the Excess Profits Tax in January 1940, by which 50 per cent of all profits above an income of Rs 36,000 was to be taxed. Big business reacted to this measure with alarm. It argued that it was a tax on capital and not on income, and would limit the flow of new capital sorely needed to finance the war industry. For the first time in their history, business organizations across the subcontinent almost took to the streets in protest. At one public meeting held on 9 February 1940 in Bombay, under the auspices of the Indian Merchants' Chamber, fifty-one chambers of commerce and industry joined hands to denounce the new tax.[46]

A number of factors further alienated big business from government. Given their support of the war effort, Indian industrialists expected to be co-opted into government committees concerned with war-time planning.[47] They believed the rapid increase in production needed to meet war-related demands required technical expertise of a kind which bureaucrats could hardly be expected to possess.[48] But to their dismay, they were completely excluded from war-time economic planning. To some extent, their grievances were addressed when, in late 1940, Viceroy Linlithgow appointed Homi Mody, a prominent Bombay businessman associated with the Tata Group,

as the Supply Member of his executive council. Further
appeasement followed in June 1941 when Nalini Ranjan
Sarkar, a Bengali businessman and politician, was inducted
as Member for Education, Health and Lands. These
appointments, to some extent, pacified business. But the
overall perception remained that there was no real desire
on the part of government for a partnership with Indian
business. This perception was confirmed by the attitude
shown during the proceedings of the Roger Mission, when
local businessmen were not invited to take part in its
deliberations, and when the mission's recommendation to
incorporate them on official bodies was not heeded either.[49]
This experience was repeated at the Eastern Group Supply
Conference. Although several representatives from FICCI
and European chambers of commerce were invited, Indian
businesspersons were excluded from all decision-making at
the conference.[50]

A further cause of discord between big business
and government arose over the so-called 'scorched
earth' policy. After the Japanese victories in late 1941,
the Allies became nervous about land attacks on India.
Consequently, the Government of India proposed the
'scorched earth' policy, which entailed the destruction
of important facilities such as port terminals, airfields,
factories, and means of transport like railways so that they
would not fall into enemy hands in case of an attack.
Big business reacted with panic to this proposal. FICCI
declared that the country's economic capacity would be
severely impaired by even a partial implementation of

such a policy. Prominent business leader G.L. Mehta
vehemently asserted that FICCI could not accept a
policy formulated by an army command that was not in
the hands of Indians. Mehta pointed out that in Russia,
from where the policy was borrowed, the 'sons of the soil'
had issued orders for its implementation. In India, the
situation was vastly different.[51] Business leaders appealed
to the Congress to take up their cause. On their persuasion,
Gandhi wrote an article in *Harijan* expressing opposition
to the policy.[52] Fortunately for big business, the 'scorched
earth' policy was not implemented, and Indian industrial
plants and equipment were spared destruction.

Still another cause for resentment was the plight of
Indian refugees from Burma after its fall to Japan. Many
of these refugees included members of the Marwari and
Chettiar business communities. When they were forced to
evacuate Burma without any assistance from the British
colonial government, there was much resentment at the
government's apathy. FICCI went so far as to allege that
the evacuation policy of the government was racist, as
preferential treatment had been given to British refugees.[53]

By 1943, big business was unanimous in its view
that the government's policies were leading to large-scale
economic disruption and suffering. This was reflected,
for example, in rampant inflation and in the shortage of
essential commodities. The government's response to
this crisis was to impose controls. Initially, trade controls
were introduced, and they included prohibition of exports
and imports to enemy countries, restriction of the flow of

specific commodities to neutral and friendly countries, and control of foreign exchange to conserve sterling resources. Trade controls were followed by commodity controls which restricted production, distribution and pricing of wheat, foodgrains, sugar and textiles, among other goods. Although business leaders recognized that a degree of control was necessary to deal with the extraordinary situation that prevailed on account of the War, they strongly disagreed with the methods used by the government in enforcing such controls, and wanted self-regulation by industry rather than coercion by the state.[54]

On Birla's initiative, Thakurdas, Lala Shri Ram, Kasturbhai and other prominent businessmen such as Haridas Madhavdas and Padampat Singhania met in March 1943 and put forth a scheme of self-regulation by the textile industry to bring down prices of cloth, yarn and cotton. It was agreed that mills would sell their output within two months of production and that wholesalers, in turn, would sell their goods within thirty days of actual receipt. The government, on its part, would legislate against storage of cloth and impose restrictions on industry manufacturing cloth beyond certain peak levels. By these measures, they felt, prices would automatically come down. The mill owners asked to be given the statutory power to make it possible for industry to control standard production, and in return, they were willing to ensure that they would provide cloth at reasonable prices.[55] This was 'substantially the same' basis of a plan worked out with Akbar Hydari, secretary of industries and civil supplies, for self-regulation of the textile industry.[56] It proved to be a great success. Within one year, prices were lowered four times, resulting in a reduction by almost 40 per cent.[57] Such government–business cooperation in the textile industry was, however, untypical if one takes an overall view of the relations between big business and government at the time, with the former becoming increasingly trenchant in its criticism of official wartime economic policies.

Many businesspersons, even while profiting from war-induced demand, had nagging doubts about what the end of World War II would bring. They especially feared the difficult transition in reconverting to peacetime production and dealing with surplus stocks. From the early months of the War, they had raised this concern at various chambers of commerce. FICCI, for instance, warned that industry must 'not be left high and dry' at the end of the War.[58] Individually, businesspersons took whatever measures they could to protect themselves. A cautious Shri Ram instructed his managers to organize war production in 'such a way that even if at any time government cancels the order, or refuses to take delivery of the goods, we shall not have much of semi-finished or finished stocks on hand'.[59] He told them of his 'bitter experience' at the end of World War I, when tent orders for lakhs of rupees were brusquely rejected. Officials refused to even meet him. 'Those who previously used to come out of their offices to see me off would not allow me to get into their offices without a previous appointment, and the appointment was never granted,' he told his managers.[60]

Although, on the surface, Indian industry benefited greatly from war-induced demand, there were underlying problems that prevented its potential from being maximized. As JRD put it, 'the limiting factor in production' was 'not money but industrial capacity and labour'.[61] Working double shifts to keep up with the booming demand for war-related goods, machinery in factories suffered immense wear and tear while the construction of new facilities ground to a halt because of restrictions on materials like cement. There was widespread labour unrest, with the working classes reeling under rising prices and scarcity of foodstuffs. Real wages did not keep pace with inflation, even though dearness allowance was introduced in December 1939. Labour shortfalls were accentuated during the 'Quit India' movement, which attracted widespread support from workers. It was apparent to all that much of the industrial expansion was only in sectors related to war demand and that other sections of Indian industry were falling behind their overseas competitors in terms of mechanization and rationalization.

Indian industry was held back in other ways too by the colonial government. No less a person than JRD had to suffer his share of disappointment. Very keen to enter aircraft production with Mosquito twin-engine fighter bombers and gliders, Tata Aircraft Limited was started for this purpose in 1942, but this plan could never take off.[62] Birla's and the Gujarati industrialist Walchand Hirachand's proposals to set up automobile plants were also rejected by the government, on the grounds that the manufacture of automobiles did not fall within the 'war effort category'.[63] This came as a bitter disappointment to Indian businessmen, and business bodies interpreted this as a deliberate attempt by the colonial government to curtail the potential of Indian industry. What added to their frustration was that even while these proposals were rejected, the ministry of supply in London commissioned General Motors to set up a car factory in India to commence production with imported parts. Denouncing the decision, Mehta said: 'While a hundred and one difficulties are suggested whenever there is any proposal for establishing a key industry by Indians, there is no hesitation in permitting such assembly plants being established when it is done by non-Indians.'[64] FICCI contended the automobile industry 'suffered postponement merely to satisfy the pressure of alien influence'[65] and even persuaded Nehru to write an article in January 1942 against the discrimination faced by Indian industry.[66] Both Birla and Hirachand had to wait till 1944 before they were given permission by the central government to raise capital for their automobile ventures.[67] Similarly, Hirachand's plan for shipbuilding was not encouraged by the government, causing still more resentment.[68]

For all these disappointments, the War, with its 'strong and direct stimulus', marked a genuine turnaround in the fortunes of Indian industry, which came confidently into its own. Even contemporary observers who were sceptical of India's potential to industrialize acknowledged that 'the experiences and developments of World War the

Second have brought about such rapid changes and such a fundamentally different economic situation, that an opportunity has hereby been created for a break with the past and for an economic reconstruction on a scale that would otherwise have been inconceivable.'[69]

By mid-1942, India had become the eighth most industrialized country in the world, moving up from twelfth position two years ago. The GDP in real terms increased by 10.6 per cent during the War years, real manufacturing output expanded by 61.6 per cent, employment soared by 59 per cent, the number of privately owned factories increased by 40 per cent, and government-owned factories by 235 per cent.[70] To astute observers such as *The Economist,* it was apparent that no less than an 'industrial revolution' was under way.[71]

2

THE STERLING BALANCE
AND INDIA'S FUTURE

From debtor to creditor

Business confidence about the future, already buoyed by the economic impact of World War II and the frenetic industrial activity that was transforming India, received a further fillip with the rapidly changing financial equation between India and Britain. At the start of World War II, India owed Britain over £360 million, a debt which it had accumulated since the mid-nineteenth century for expenditure incurred on a number of counts on its behalf in England.[1] During World War II, Indian factories churned out war materials ranging from boots to armaments, the army expanded to 2.5 million men, while almost 200,000 civil and semi-military administrators were recruited to sustain the war effort. A fortuitous outcome of all this war-related activity was that India grew out of debt.[2] The heavy volume of defence-related expenditure pared India's debt in two years, from £360 million to £240 million in 1940–41. Till 1943, the accumulating sterling balance was used to offset the long-standing debt of India. However, once India's debt was wiped out, Britain began to pay for all its war-related expenditure in India in sterling. This sterling amount was kept in the Bank of England in London and rupee notes were issued against it.[3]

Before the War, no one could have imagined that India would manage to repay a debt accumulated over three quarters of a century in less than three years. 'India has completed the transition from a debtor to a creditor country and extinguished within the brief space of three years accumulation of . . . its public indebtedness to the United Kingdom,' declared Sir Jeremy Raisman, finance member of the viceroy's executive council.[4] Even more amazing was the huge £1.3 billion balance that India amassed in the years thereafter.[5] This dramatic accumulation of sterling balance revolutionized India's financial relationship with Britain and saw her emerging as a creditor with a substantial portfolio. By the end of the War, India was one of Britain's largest creditors, along with Egypt.

Pinning hopes on the sterling balance

The rebalancing of financial relations between Britain and India was keenly followed by Indian business leaders who had been keeping an eye on the sterling–rupee movement since World War I. At that time, it had been fervently hoped that India would be granted more financial autonomy in return for the generous war loans raised in the Bombay money market for the British war effort. Many Indian business leaders were excited by the steady accumulation of sterling reserves with the Government of India in lieu of payments made for war purchases. They saw this reserve as an invaluable source for funding industrial expansion and economic reconstruction after the War.

The lead was taken by Birla who, after a close reading of the Reserve Bank of India statements, began, as early as in 1941, to urge his friends in the commercial world to take cognizance of these developments.[6] Birla was excited but at the same time apprehensive. On the one hand, he was excited about the sterling credit balance that India was building up with its war effort—funds which could potentially be used for industrial development. On the other hand, he was apprehensive about the uncertainty surrounding the future of sterling balances. Causes for worry included Allied reverses in Singapore, Burma and Malaya, and the Japanese threat of invasion in north-east India. If Britain and its Allies lost the War, the sterling could well suffer the same fate as the German mark after World War I. Any depreciation of the sterling would reduce India's sterling balances and adversely affect the value of the Indian rupee, which was backed entirely by the sterling.[7] Another worry was that as its debts mounted, Britain could try to manipulate the terms of its agreement with India on war payments. 'Everything is being done behind the scenes. Commercial community or non-official world has got no knowledge of what is happening [*sic*],' he noted. To make matters worse, Indian nationalist leaders had 'very little knowledge' about these issues. He thus urged his friends that 'it is obviously our business to educate them'.[8]

Birla prodded influential colleagues who were on the board of the Reserve Bank of India, especially Thakurdas, Kasturbhai, Calcutta businessman Badridas Goenka and Shri Ram, to take on the role of 'custodians of our finances' and to pursue the issue.[9] 'The question is very simple,' he told Thakurdas. 'England is our debtor. And we must make a simple demand that our credits should be fully safeguarded.'[10] Although Thakurdas recognized the potential use of the sterling balance, he believed that the time was not opportune to press the issue and reprimanded Birla for 'asking for the moon'.[11] He feared that publicly raising the issue in the midst of the War could backfire and result in a reworking of the Defence of India agreement, with the risk of an increase in the allocation of war expenses to India.[12] Birla found it hard convincing his peers. Months later, in March 1943, an exasperated Birla told a like-minded industrialist: 'I fear you are knocking your head against a steel wall. The industrialist and specially Big Business is in deep slumber and they have no desire to stir up at all. . . . I have been fighting for the last three years to persuade them to take some attitude about the sterling resources, and so far they have not even decided as to what to do.'[13]

It took a series of disappointments, including imposition of Excess Profits Tax (*see Chapter 1*), the sidelining of Indian interests in high-powered committees, the looming threat of a 'scorched earth' policy vis-à-vis Japan, and the appointment of the British business representative Sir Edward Benthall as member of the viceroy's executive council to galvanize different segments of big business. Further, the breakdown of negotiations after the failure of the Cripps Mission, followed by the 'Quit India' movement led by Mahatma Gandhi in 1942 and its violent suppression by the Raj, all led to a situation which Kasturbhai described to his close friend Guy Coleridge in the following words: 'There has never been in India before such a feeling of resentment, bitterness and at the same time hopelessness at the attitude adopted by the people in England.' He defended Gandhi as being 'quite right in demanding that something ought to be done immediately to catch the imagination of the people, by making them feel that it was their war and not the war of the Britishers'. The disillusionment of business knew no bounds: 'Take the utter callousness of the Government in piling up sterling resources in England. Would not any businessman in India feel that these resources ought to be set off against British investments in India, so that there will be a better security for our currency and a better hope for the future,' said Kasturbhai.[14]

From late 1942 till early 1943, FICCI, the voice of Indian business, took every opportunity to raise the sterling question. Individual business leaders, especially Thakurdas, Kasturbhai, Shroff and, needless to say, Birla led a public campaign to demand the unfreezing of sterling balances. They continued this campaign through their writings, within official bodies in which they were involved, and at various business associations.

Funding post-war reconstruction and industrialization

The sterling reserve was seen by many within Indian business as providing a potential source of funding for post-war economic reconstruction as well as for the establishment of key heavy industries like shipbuilding in the country. During the war years, whatever little Indian industry existed was commandeered to churn out war supplies for the Allied cause at a frenetic pace. This caused enormous wear and tear of plants and machinery. It was clear that restoration of equipment to even pre-war levels would require substantial import of capital goods. The textile sector, for instance, was particularly badly hit, because not only was most of its machinery damaged due to excessive production, even equipment, wherever intact, was obsolete, since most of it had been installed prior to World War I. At the very least, textile mills needed to replace most of their plants.[15] This, in turn, implied huge capital goods imports, as India barely had any such industries, other than the newly incorporated Birla Textile Machinery Corporation of 1941.

Capital goods imports would be needed not only for the reconstruction of existing industries, but would also be required to set up greenfield industries like shipbuilding, locomotives, automobiles, chemicals and machine tools. Business leaders expected the post-war economic policy to emphasize the development of heavy industries. Implementing such a policy would necessarily hinge on large-scale imports of capital goods that could be purchased using the sterling balance. Such industrial development would enable India to become 'a strong and self-reliant national economy', even 'an arsenal of the East'.[16] '(A) development programme must command the first place on India's post-war plans,' declared Thakurdas in 1944. 'It will make a very great difference,' he went on to say in a press statement, 'to the burden of the cost of such a programme whether it is financed from India's accumulated sterling balances or from fresh savings.'[17] For Birla, the sterling balance was no less than the 'life and death' of future industrialization. His *Eastern Economist* called it 'our camel's hump to ferry us over the weak waterless desert of our First Five-Year Plan'.[18] Thus, all ideas about India's future development plans crucially hinged on utilization of the sterling balance.

Machinery and capital goods could be purchased from not only Britain, but also from other developed countries like the US, since the sterling was convertible into other hard currencies. The sterling balance was thus seen as having the capability of fulfilling India's future needs concomitant with rapid industrial development—a path that India hoped to embark upon following the War.[19] Not only could the sterling balance be used to buy goods, it could also be used to pay for the much-needed technical expertise from Britain and the US. This view found widespread support in official circles.[20]

Many business leaders also hoped to draw on the sterling balance for the acquisition of British companies by Indian managing agencies. Such acquisitions would include European companies registered in India, as also those registered elsewhere but operating in India. In this way, sterling investments in tea, rubber plantations, mines, oil, coal and jute could be acquired and brought under Indian control. In 1942, Indian business chambers suggested that the sterling reserve could be used to acquire foreign-held debentures of public bodies like municipalities and improvement trusts, and public utility and transport companies.[21] Further, British commercial rupee investments in shipbuilding and in plants built for war purposes could be transferred to Indian hands. Thus, the sterling balance would enable key sectors of the economy to move from British to Indian control.

Finally, many business leaders were optimistic that the repatriated sterling debt would leave the Indian rupee 'fundamentally stronger' than it was before the War. Thakurdas hoped that, freed from the 'apron strings' of the sterling, independent India's monetary policy would promote local agriculture and industry without having to be concerned about its effect on the servicing of foreign debt. India's gold and dollar reserves would be built up with the sterling. Thus, the sterling assets would 'prove a source of considerable strength to the Indian rupee' in the post-war scenario.[22]

The flip side: apprehensions about the sterling balance

It is noteworthy, however, that the optimism engendered by the rapidly accumulating sterling balance was tempered by a deep sense of uncertainty among business leaders. To begin with, the future course of the War remained unclear, and the worry was that any reverses in Allied fortunes would result in a depreciation of the sterling and a loss of its standing as an international currency. To avoid this risk, business leaders asked for an assurance that the sterling balance not be subjected to depreciation, as this would then not reduce its foreign currency equivalent. In March 1943, FICCI demanded an undertaking that 'the British Government shall compensate the Reserve Bank of India for all its sterling holdings to the extent of such depreciation'.[23] If the debt was to be expressed in gold units rather than in pounds sterling, then depreciation could be ruled out.

Within the Reserve Bank board of directors, Thakurdas tried hard to push through a resolution that any depreciation in the value of the sterling would not affect the overall value of the balance. This provoked a strong rebuke from the bank's governor that such a move 'would enable India both to eat its inflationary cake and have it too'.[24] However, Thakurdas was able to persuade the board to secure an assurance from the Government of India that the sterling balance would be available whenever needed. The board also recommended to the government that it draw up a programme of post-war reconstruction, including provision for working capital and other ways and means of financing the anticipated industrial development.

One way to protect India's sterling balance against a possible depreciation was to get the British government to agree to its convertibility. The pound had been inconvertible since the outbreak of the War, when a system of exchange control was put in place with an eye on mobilizing external assets and income.[25] Allowing it to become convertible would allow freer trade since India would not have to restrict itself to imports from Britain. India could also use its sterling balance to finance imports from the US and other 'hard currency' areas. Business leaders thus made the case that 'India should not only have the choice but also the wherewithal to make her purchase of capital goods, plants, machinery etc. in the cheapest and best markets of the world'.[26]

Business leaders were especially perturbed when they learnt that other colonial sterling balance holders placed in a similar situation were being protected. For example, Argentina, like India, had built up a substantial sterling balance, amounting to almost £80 million by December 1944. Britain undertook to shelter Argentina by a gold guarantee scheme that protected it from devaluation of the pound. Likewise, South Africa's sterling dues had been linked to their gold value by the British. That Indian reserves were not being treated on par and stood exposed to risk was seen to be grossly unjust. Big business demanded a similar guarantee in gold for India's sterling balance, as had been given to Argentina and South Africa.[27] Some business leaders even suggested linking it to the UK price index if guaranteeing the sterling balance against gold was not possible.[28] 'Our sterling wealth should be fully secured, if by no other means at least by relating it to the present UK price index number.'[29]

Another widespread concern was that the balance may get frittered away in maintaining the rupee–sterling ratio, a warning many economists had been making. Thakurdas seized every opportunity he got to show how, during World War I, over £55 million pounds of sterling reserve had been 'dissipated' within a few months in a bid to maintain the exchange value of the rupee, which had fallen to one shilling, in the interest of British imports and to continue remittances to Britain on favourable terms.[30] Thus, business leaders were on guard to ensure that the sterling balance was not treated as a currency reserve, but as a loan given to the British.

A constant worry for business leaders was that the terms of the Defence Expenditure Plan might be clandestinely reworked. Rumours about this cropped up time and again, but they became particularly 'alarming' as the War spread to the Middle East and to other theatres, especially Burma. It was feared that the 'reconquering of Burma' and the defence of Iraq and Iran would all be debited to India. Hence, business leaders felt an urgency to resolve the sterling issue. A worried FICCI president went public about such fears in 1942. In a press statement he warned that the rising sterling balance 'might be appropriated on the plea of equal sacrifices for war effort'.[31] He demanded a reassurance from the government to the public that these were baseless rumours.[32]

Business leaders were very concerned that decisions impacting India's sterling reserves may be made without their knowledge. They demanded that all sterling-related discussions should take place in the public domain and that non-official and commercial opinion be heard. It was deplorable, stated FICCI President G.L. Mehta, that India was not in a position to determine the terms of its sterling payment or to safeguard its reserves. He demanded that there should be no clandestine discussions and that all decisions must involve members of the central board of directors of the Reserve Bank which included business representatives.[33] FICCI kept an alert eye on all sterling balance-related matters. In March 1943, it raised objections to a government scheme that proposed using the sterling balance to make future payments towards pensions and provident fund payouts, arguing that the reserves needed to be used 'more profitably and beneficially' for economic reconstruction.[34]

Insiders in the political establishment knew such fears were not unfounded. As the War enveloped new countries and expenses reached staggering proportions, the British Treasury and the Bank of England both started to quietly push for a renegotiation of India's war-time obligations and the related financial arrangements about payments.

The Bank of England was particularly unhappy at not having been involved in the drawing up of the Defence Expenditure Plan. In early 1942, with sterling balances inching towards 200 million, the Bank of England, with the support of the Treasury benches, started asking for a new settlement in India on the principle of 'equal sacrifice'. The Government of India, however, had a different view, since it feared alienating Indians sympathetic to the Allied cause. Sir Jeremy Raisman, finance member of the viceroy's executive council, warned the Treasury in July 1942 that any change in the settlement would 'alienate the commercial classes, which had hitherto co-operated well in the War effort'.[35] Keeping in mind the Japanese advance and the collapse of Singapore and Burma, Indian cooperation became even more strategically important. Declared Raisman: 'India is just not in the mood to give anything away as yet, and until the mood changes sterling will accumulate . . . The days are past when India can with impunity be coerced against her will in almost anything. Her nuisance value is enormous.'[36]

However, strong voices within British official circles continued to argue that a resettling of the terms of defence payments was needed. In the summer of 1944, no less a person than John Maynard Keynes himself, then an adviser to the British Treasury, publicly advocated in *The Economist* a revision of the financial settlement between Britain and India. He claimed that the existing arrangement, as it stood, had unfavourable repercussions on India's economy and aggravated inflation. For quite some time, Keynes had been demanding that the Treasury and the Bank of England should tell India frankly that its sterling balances would not be at its free disposal after the War.

Both Thakurdas and Birla strongly admonished the British economist for asking for a renegotiation of the financial settlement and for suggesting a scaling down of the sterling reserve. Thakurdas termed Keynes's assertion that a revised financial settlement would not be a real burden on the people of India as 'fallacious, if not also cynical'.[37] He further noted: 'The choice which Mr Keynes is offering is between voluntary reduction of our sterling balances or compulsory reduction by way of depreciation in the value of the sterling. In brief, India is being asked to commit financial suicide in order to save herself from financial slaughter. Comment on this is needless,' said Thakurdas.[38] On his part, Birla reproached Keynes for indulging in 'loose talk'; Keynes's arguments were no less than an 'insult to Indian intelligence' and 'India need not be taught elementary economics'. Birla blamed the government's expenditure on the War for the sufferings and the famine in Bengal. He took the opportunity to reaffirm the business view that the sterling reserve was 'the only hope to raise India's standard' of living as it would help buy the much-needed capital goods to build up India's economy after the War.[39]

Businesspersons vs economists

Unlike business leaders, economists were not so optimistic about the future of the sterling. They questioned whether the accumulating sterling balance could even be viewed as India's reserves. The eminent Bombay economist and London School of Economics (LSE) alumnus C.N. Vakil, for instance, refused to even call the accumulating sterling hoard 'balance', arguing that it was by no means 'an unfettered bank balance'.[40] The reserve, he believed, would be used to maintain the value of the rupee at the exchange rate of 1s 6d (one shilling and six pence), as the British desired, and would be 'utilized for a currency purpose and with a currency effect'. The most Vakil was willing to concede was that the sterling assets 'may have some uncertain and lower values in goods for this country at a future date [sic].'[41]

What worried many Indian economists most was the rising inflation, which they blamed on the sterling. Vakil was the first to draw attention to the link between the sterling and rising inflation. Armed with an impressive array of data, Vakil blamed inflation on the British government's rupee expenditure against which India was being paid in sterling. He argued that, even though the payment was being made in London in sterling, the rupee finance required for initial purchases inevitably necessitated the issuing of additional rupee notes against the sterling. This increase in note circulation stimulated inflation. Criticizing the inflation induced by the excessive printing of money became the economists' 'stock-in-trade' for the next few years.[42] In the course of this polemic, the possibilities that the sterling build-up offered in terms of facilitating India's future development were ignored.[43]

In April 1943, in a somewhat exceptional move, twenty leading economists, including Vakil, B.R. Shenoy, V.G. Kale, A. Wadia, D.R. Gadgil and J.J. Anjaria, issued a public statement on the recent economic policy of the Government of India. They claimed that 'the rapid rise in the general price level during the past two years and the enormous expansion of currency in India are, we feel, causally related'. They pointed out that a deficit-induced 'inflationary spiral' was 'already at work', and that this was 'the most disastrous type of inflation'. Basically, the Indian government's expenditure was more than its revenues because of the system of war finances under which the British and Allied purchases were being paid for.[44] To address this expenditure–revenue gap, the government was resorting to deficit-financing by issuing more currency. Not often given to making public statements, the economists' 'manifesto' garnered attention from official quarters and led the Government of India to introduce early anti-inflationary measures.[45]

In contrast to the economists, business leaders were at pains to persuade the authorities to delink the sterling reserves from inflation. From diverse public forums, they claimed that rising prices were simply caused by shortages, not inflation, and that prices could be controlled by stimulating supplies. In this view, the price rise was due to shortages and problems in distribution that could be remedied by increasing the production of goods. Business associations across India passed resolutions on the need to increase production to deal with the inflationary situation.

Some business leaders openly critiqued the economists. For instance, M.L. Shah, president of the Calcutta-based Indian Chamber of Commerce, criticized the economists for their 'academic proposals to combat an inflationary spiral which hardly exists with methods borrowed from other countries which are not in consonance with our conditions and might react prejudicially on our national economy'.[46] The 'scarcity' explanation was commonly used by many chambers of commerce, so much so that Vakil almost felt a 'systematic propaganda' campaign was under way to counter his arguments.[47]

Birla took the view that the economists were 'inspired more by textbooks than the verdict of those who with their experience of actual production knew what could be achieved and what would be the result of this neglect'.[48] In a boldly titled pamphlet, 'Inflation or Scarcity?', published in February 1943, he countered that there was no inflation. There had been, he stated, an 'expansion' of currency, which was not responsible for the rise in prices.[49] Rising prices was due to the scarcity of commodities, and Birla strongly advocated for a policy of rapid production of consumer goods. In his view, inflation was 'hardly the root cause of our trouble which in reality arises from an insufficiency of goods for the consumption of the public'. Pointing out the increased volume of government purchases and price trends, he argued that the effect of the War was eating up goods, and only increased production could check the rise in prices. As he put it: 'No amount of currency deflation or curtailment of prices or freezing of prices will solve the problem of scarcity. The only solution is to produce more food and more cloth and more of other consumption goods.'[50]

While there was unanimity amongst business leaders and various chambers of commerce that production needed to be increased, not all businesspersons absolved the sterling of blame for inflation. Kasturbhai, for instance, agreed with the economists' view on the causal relation between expansion of currency supply and inflation. Birla pointed out that he was 'on the wrong track' and chided him quite brusquely: 'Some economists, who never produced goods worth five rupees in their life think that increase in production is not possible. I have nothing but contempt for their opinion. But if a businessman goes on talking in the language of pedantics, it could not be excused.'[51] In a scenario such as this, few business leaders were willing to take a public stance on the inflation debate.

One economist who found himself on the same side as business leaders was Lokanathan. He asserted that 'the business community was in substance correct in arguing that the true remedy consisted in an increase in production'.[52] He felt his economist colleagues, by making a direct causal relation between currency expansion and prices, had 'unduly simplified the issue and exaggerated the monetary aspect of inflation'. He accused his peers of being 'quantity theorists' and for looking only at the 'purely monetary methods of price control'. More currency supply, he argued, did not necessarily mean higher prices.

All it meant was that there was a greater need for proactive management of the currency.[53]

What happened to the sterling balance?[54]

At Independence, India's sterling reserves stood at £1134 million; this was after paying its share to Pakistan, and paying Britain for military stores left behind, for pension annuities, for commodity imports and capital outflows. Alongside, the Government of India drew freely from the sterling reserve for imports of food, and of capital and intermediate goods, while about a third of the gold value of the reserves was extinguished by the sterling's devaluation in September 1949. Hence, by the end of 1949, India's sterling balance had been reduced to £621 million. The existing level of sterling, however, in the words of economic historian G. Balachandran, still remained 'a comfortable cushion for the foreseeable future'. An interim agreement signed between India and Britain in August 1947 divided the balance into two accounts—'a current account' (Account No. 1) and a 'blocked account' (Account No. 2). A working balance of £30 million was in the current account, and it was agreed that an additional £35 million of convertible sterling would be released for the year. The blocked account could only be used to pay for certain items, such as surplus military stores, pension liabilities and the financing of capital outflows from India to the rest of the sterling area.

Another interim agreement signed in January 1948 saw the release of £18 million for a six-month period. Thereafter, a three-year agreement was signed in end-1948, by which there were to be no releases for a year, but after that, a release of £40 million in each of the following two years and anticipatory drawings, if necessary. In 1951, after much discussion on the quantum of sterling releases amidst British allegations of overdrawing by India, a six-year agreement was finally signed. This provided for release of £35 million each year, with an immediate transfer of £310 million from Account No. 2 to Account No. 1, on the condition that it could not be drawn upon, except in consultation with the British government. At the end of six years, any balance in Account No. 2 was to go into Account No. 1. This paved the way for the unblocking of the Indian sterling balance, and the matter ended most amicably.

3

THE AUTHORS OF THE PLAN

Introduction

On Friday, 11 December 1942, the morning's newspapers, as in the last three and a half years, were full of war news. Though the German and Japanese campaigns had weakened over the course of 1942, there were no signs that the War was coming to an end. Just a few days earlier, on 2 December, it was officially confirmed that 2 million Jews had been killed in Germany and 5 million more were in danger of extermination.

The domestic situation too was marked by unease and disquiet. The 'Quit India' movement, initiated by Mahatma Gandhi on 9 August 1942, had unleashed an 'unprecedented and countrywide wave of mass fury'. In the cities, it had elicited massive demonstrations by industrial workers, including widespread strikes, close-downs and clashes with the police and army. There were short strikes in the Birla and Shri Ram cotton mills in Delhi, while Kasturbhai's textile mill in Ahmedabad suffered a protracted three-month strike. The Tata steel plant too witnessed a record thirteen-day closure during which labour declared they would not resume work until a national government had been formed.[1] All told, it took the British fifty-seven and a half battalions to suppress the protests. Although by December, open resistance had lessened, the movement went underground and began manifesting itself in terrorist activities by the youth. The entire nationalist leadership was still in jail, and those leaders who had managed to evade imprisonment, such as Jayaprakash Narayan and Aruna Asaf Ali, were leading the underground movement. No resolution of the political stalemate seemed in sight, even as the British authorities continued to put pressure on Indian businessmen to carry on supporting the war effort by expanding capacity in different sectors. On the morning of 11 December too, the newspapers had talked about the need to increase the manufacture of chemicals.

It was against such a backdrop of troubled headlines, with uncertainty about India's economic future weighing heavily on their minds, that five of the country's leading businessmen—Thakurdas, JRD, Kasturbhai, G.D. Birla and Shri Ram—and two economists, John Matthai and A.D. Shroff, trained at London School of Economics (LSE), decided to meet at the historic premises of Bombay House, the headquarters of the Tata group, to talk things over.

Of the five businessmen, Thakurdas and JRD were based in Bombay, and Kasturbhai was from Ahmedabad; Birla's firm was headquartered in Calcutta while Shri Ram operated from Delhi. So it was a fairly pan-Indian grouping, although there was no representative from the south. The idea for such a conclave had originated a couple of months earlier, in October, quite by chance, when Birla and JRD met in Delhi. In view of the dramatic economic changes that India was undergoing as a result of its involvement in the War, both men felt that a 'small committee of industrialists aided by eminent economists' should come together to formulate an 'agreed programme' on the post-war economy. Two obvious names for inclusion were those of Thakurdas and Kasturbhai, both of whom had been actively engaged in commercial and public life for at least three decades. Just a few days before the 11 December meeting, JRD invited Shri Ram, a choice Birla was not confident about but nonetheless went along with.[2] JRD also roped in three 'in-house experts'—John Matthai, A.D. Shroff and, later, Ardeshir Dalal, while Birla enlisted the help of Lokanathan, the newly appointed editor of the *Eastern Economist*, a journal he was hoping to model on the London-based *The Economist*.

Disparate in age and temperament, these nine men were, however, united in their concern over the possible contours of the post-war economic landscape. A brief look at their ideas and achievements till 1942—when they sat down together to draft a blueprint for India's development—is warranted.

The Bombay businessmen

The two Bombay-based businessmen, sixty-three-year-old Thakurdas and thirty-eight-year-old JRD, were the senior-most and the youngest, respectively, in the group. Thakurdas was easily the most illustrious of the group and widely considered the 'doyen of the commercial community in India'.[3] In 1942, he was on the board of almost seventy companies, including many from the Tata group, without having a controlling interest in any of them. His directorships included those of banks—he was on the board of the Reserve Bank of India since its establishment in April 1935—and of companies spanning insurance, cement, iron and steel, transport, hydroelectric power, radio and telegraph, and at least thirty-two textile mills.[4] He was very active in the commercial organizations of western India, as also in the foremost all-India business body, FICCI. During his four-decade public career he had held a number of prestigious official positions, including sheriff of Bombay, been honoured with various titles, including a knighthood, and had been nominated to the Bombay legislative council and assembly, and elected to the central legislative assembly. Not surprisingly, he enjoyed unrivalled prestige as a front-ranking leader of big business in India.

Thakurdas's career dated back to 1901 when he joined his family's cotton, oilseed, rice trading and commission firm, Narandas Rajaram & Co. A Hindu Gujarati of the Kapol Bania caste, Thakurdas joined the family firm after he graduated from Elphinstone College in Bombay. As a young, educated trader, he gained a reputation for introducing 'modern business methods' in the family firm, which enabled its entry into European cotton-broking circles and brought it prestigious brokerships, such as those of Sassoon and Company and Killick Nixon and Company.[5] Thakurdas soon became well known amongst Bombay's cotton traders for his championship of anti-adulteration, thanks to his public opposition of 'watering and mixing' in raw cotton, a practice that had tarnished the standing of many of the city's selling agents.[6] This enhanced his reputation amongst the city marketers and, at the young age of twenty-eight, he was selected as the first vice president of the Bombay Indian Merchants Chamber and Bureau (later known as the Indian Merchants Chamber), then the largest body of cotton traders in western India.

From a young age, Thakurdas showed a deep interest in public life. In 1911, at the time of famine in parts of Bombay Presidency, he served as secretary and treasurer of the famine relief fund. This brought him his first official honour, the Kasier-i-Hind medal.[7] Soon thereafter, in 1916, he was nominated to the Bombay legislative council and, later, to the Bombay legislative assembly. Other honours followed, including Companion of the Order of the Indian Empire in 1919, appointment as sheriff of Bombay a year later, and knighthood in 1923.

Early in his career, Thakurdas had understood the importance of solidarity and unity amongst the commercial community. In 1921, he founded the Indian

Central Cotton Committee, an association of cotton merchants and industrialists from across the subcontinent. He was also an active member of the East India Cotton Association, established in 1922, and was regarded its 'reigning Mughal' for over thirty-five years. He had also held official positions at the Bombay Cotton Exchange, including a term as its president. These were all influential positions, considering that by the 1920s, Bombay was, after New York and Liverpool, the third largest cotton market in the world and the largest in Asia. Most significantly, Thakurdas, together with Birla, played a leading role in the formation of FICCI, the first apex association that brought all Indian commercial organizations under one common umbrella.

By the late 1920s, Thakurdas was a leading figure in the Bombay business community and was known to be close to both Indian and European traders and marketers as well as to local industrialists. He had a reputation for 'robust common sense' and 'courageous thinking and speaking'. By now, he had started to work with economists and businesspersons such as C.N. Vakil, K.T. Shah, P.A. Wadia, G.N. Joshi and A.D. Shroff to articulate a comprehensive critique of British currency policies vis-à-vis India and the rupee–sterling ratio. This was an issue first raised by Bombay businessmen in the 1890s, but it became more central in Indian–European business relations post-World War I. In forums dedicated to the cause, such as the Indian Currency League set up in 1926 and local business interests, with Thakurdas and Shroff in the forefront, argued against the raising of the rupee–sterling ratio to 1/6.[8] Thakurdas had also been a member of the Royal Commission on Indian Currency and Finance (the Hilton-Young Commission) of 1925–26, on whose report he had signed a note of dissent. Thakurdas single-mindedly pursued this issue in various political and business forums through the 1920s. So well articulated and effective was his critique and also that of his Bombay colleagues' that almost all of India's economic ills came to be blamed on the 'high ratio' adopted after the War.

In 1924, Thakurdas was nominated by the Indian Merchants Chamber to the Central Legislative Assembly as a representative of commercial interests. His tenure coincided with that of Birla's and Kasturbhai's, with whom he developed a close friendship. Thakurdas, Birla and Kasturbhai were uncompromising critics of British economic policies in India. In 1930, when the Cotton Industries Protection Bill, which created differential duties on British and non-British goods, was passed, Thakurdas resigned his seat in the central assembly, as did Birla. Between 1930 and 1932, Thakurdas was appointed as a delegate to the Second and Third Round Table Conferences in London, and served on the joint parliamentary committee for drafting a new constitution for India.

Amidst these years of active public life, it was economic concerns that animated Thakurdas's politics. As he put it: 'I am interested in politics only to the extent that politics reacts on economics.'[9] Thakurdas was no loyalist of the Raj, and while he appears to be a 'reluctant nationalist', he was unwavering in his support of indigenous capital and enterprise. His disappointment with the Government of India's position on a number of economic issues, especially the currency question, had convinced him that he needed to take a stand on political matters. As he observed in 1929: 'We can no more separate our politics from our economics than make the sun and the moon stand.'[10] Although he vehemently critiqued the Raj's economic policies, the Gandhian-style of agitational politics that was overtaking the city of Bombay in the post-war years also held no appeal for Thakurdas. He had opposed Gandhi's first Non Co-operation Movement of 1920 and was a key member of the anti-non-cooperation committee set up by industrialists such as Dorabji Tata. Thakurdas had served as one of its two honorary secretaries and was widely credited with raising much of the funding for the committee.[11] The Gandhian agitation had convinced him that non-cooperation should be eradicated 'root and branch' and the masses brought to 'sanity and sober common sense'.[12] Yet, a few years later in 1929, when some pro-government industrialists attempted to form a capitalist association in the legislative assembly along with representatives of European business, Thakurdas objected because he saw an inherent clash between indigenous and foreign business interests.

Like many other business leaders, Thakurdas shared a close personal relationship with the Mahatma. Since their first meeting in 1920 at a common friend's home in Gamdevi in Bombay, Gandhi had taken steps to nurture this relationship and often visited Thakurdas's home during trips to Bombay. Thakurdas too was happy to help with Gandhi's constructive campaigns and served as an adviser to his All India Village Industries Association. However, he maintained a distance from Gandhi's agitational style of politics. In 1930, he opposed the Civil Disobedience Movement and, along with his friend Birla, tried to act as a mediator between the Congress and the government.[13] These were difficult phases in Thakurdas's public career, when he did not want to break relations with government officials or spoil his personal rapport with Gandhi even while articulating his opposition to the Mahatma's style of politics. In the 1930s, a matter of much concern to Thakurdas and others had been the emerging dominance of Nehru within the Congress, especially after his election as party president in 1936. Nehru's avowedly leftist stance worried Thakurdas, and he joined twenty-one Bombay-based businesspersons, including A.D. Shroff, to put together a 'manifesto' critiquing Nehru's socialist views.[14]

Since the outbreak of World War II, Thakurdas had worked closely with Birla in trying to bring about a political reconciliation between the Congress and the government. As Gandhi was inching towards another confrontation, Thakurdas tried hard to persuade the Mahatma against it. He spent an hour with him on the morning of 8 August 1942, the day before the All India Congress Committee formally adopted the 'Quit India' resolution. He met Gandhi again in the evening at Birla House in Bombay, where Gandhi was staying, to persuade him to change his mind. He was sorely disappointed when Gandhi remained unmoved, and later blamed the Mahatma for landing the country in a 'mess'.[15] Though he opposed Gandhi's political style, in the months thereafter he began to openly align himself with the nationalist leadership.

In contrast to Thakurdas, who had a long public career, J.R.D. Tata, 'Jeh' to his friends, was somewhat new to the world of business and politics. He had taken over as chairman of Tata Sons just four years earlier, in July 1938, after the unexpected demise of his predecessor, Sir Nowroji Saklatwala.[16] JRD's influence, at this point in time, stemmed from the prestige he had as head of the 'first family' of Indian business, with an almost 100-year history. The Tata group had only recently held lavish celebrations to mark the birth centenary of its founder.[17]

When JRD came to the helm of the family business, the group had fourteen major companies, many in basic industries such as steel, textiles and oil, which required long gestation periods and large sums of investment. With over 75,000 workers on its rolls, the group's combined sales by 1939 were estimated at Rs 280 crore.[18] The Tatas were also well-known philanthropists and were held in high esteem in official circles and within the larger commercial community. Deeply conscious of this heritage, JRD was very 'driven by the fact that there was Jamsetji Tata in my life and that is what urged me to do things, to keep wanting to justify myself'.[19]

In early 1942, JRD was still learning the ropes of Bombay's commercial world. Born in Paris in 1904, he had shuttled between Paris and Bombay during his childhood. His mother, Pauline Suzanne Genevieve, was a French national and his father, R.D. Tata, was a first cousin of Jamsetji Nusserwanji, founder of the house of Tatas and a partner in Tata Sons. R.D. Tata had been with the Tatas from the 1870s, when it was still just a medium-sized textile firm. After Jamsetji's demise, his son Dorabji, and R.D. Tata pushed for the launch of Tata Hydro-electric Power Supply in 1911, marking the group's transition from the cotton industry to hydroelectric power and, finally, to steel (steel was first produced on a commercial scale in 1913). JRD himself was then being schooled in Paris, after which he was drafted for a year into the French Army. He had hoped to study in Cambridge, but the unexpected demise of his father in 1926 meant he had to shoulder the family responsibility. He was appointed a permanent director of Tata Sons. He had, however, already embarked on this career two years earlier, when he had become an apprentice in Tata Steel in 1924 and moved back to India. Much of his job consisted of assisting John Peterson, who was director in charge of Tata Steel. In these early years in Bombay, JRD felt 'a little more of a Frenchman than an Indian', but gave up his French citizenship in 1929.

JRD's personal passion was flying. This passion went back to his childhood when his neighbour, Louis Bleriot, became the first man to fly across the English Channel in 1909.[20] In 1929, after JRD undertook a twenty-five-minute

flight, he earned an aviator certificate and became the first
pilot to have so qualified in India. In 1930, he flew solo from
Karachi to Paris. In October 1932, JRD landed in a Puss
Moth at Bombay's Juhu airport, carrying mail from Karachi
via Ahmedabad.[21] From 1929 onwards, he ceaselessly
lobbied the British to allow the Tatas to enter aviation. In
1932, Tata Aviation was inaugurated, and five years later,
Tata Airlines took off. Completing the cycle, Tata Aircraft
was started in March 1942 to make airplanes.[22] Perhaps
the most cosmopolitan among Indian businessmen, JRD
was always sensitive to world developments and welcomed
foreign advisers and technicians.

In his politics, JRD was inclined to follow the Tata
Sons tradition. His predecessor, Dorabji, had leaned
closely towards the British colonial government. Dorabji
was instrumental, along with other Bombay-based
businessmen, including Thakurdas, in setting up the anti-
non-cooperation committee that sought to counter the
Congress's agitational politics of 1920–22. A few years
after JRD assumed the reins of the Tata empire, he was
a key figure in trying to set up a capitalist association
in the central legislature in 1929 in cooperation with
European interests. The Tata faction was also considered
the 'backbone of Bombay Mill-Owners association', which
was close to the liberals, the old Congress 'moderates', and
opposed to the Gandhian mode of politics. Prominent
Tata men stood openly against the Congress's agitation
of 1930.[23] The Tatas even remained aloof from FICCI
till 1937, when JRD joined the organization—a strategic

move probably prompted by the fact that by then the Congress was in power in the provinces, and membership in a nationalist business organization like FICCI could be of potential benefit.

Thakurdas and JRD had a long familial relationship. Thakurdas had been appointed by JRD's predecessor, Dorabji, as a director of important Tata firms such as Tata Iron and Steel Co. and Tata Hydro-Electric Power Supply Co., and was regarded as a senior whose sage counsel was sought at difficult times. He had even intervened on behalf of the group with official authorities at times of need. In political matters, Thakurdas and the Tata elders often came together on certain key points such as the currency question in the 1920s and, later, during opposition to Nehru's radical statements in 1936. Of late, however, they were beginning to drift apart, with the Tatas remaining close to the liberals and the old Congress moderates, and Thakurdas becoming much more openly critical of the colonial government's economic policies and moving closer to the nationalist leadership, although he too was not willing to align himself openly with Gandhi's confrontational politics till the 1940s.

The other barons

Ghanshyamdas Birla was the political strategist of the group. In 1942, at the age of forty-eight, he helmed his family's business that ranked second to the Tatas in terms of the number of companies in its fold, though not in terms of capital investment. The Birla group's interests lay in cotton, jute, cement and sugar, and it was on the verge of entering the paper industry and, most significantly, textile machinery.[24]

Birla belonged to the Maheshwari sub-caste of the Marwari trading community. The family business had originated with interests in opium speculation, forward trading in several commodities such as cotton piece-goods, wheat, rapeseed and silver, and brokerage in the jute and gunny trade. Windfall profits during World War I from hedge transactions in raw jute and gunny, and speculative operations in silver and jute stocks led Birla to boldly venture into the European-dominated jute manufacturing. Soon, with support from his brothers, he led the family business in making the transition from old-style trading to modern industry, and the Birla group diversified into cotton textiles, sugar mills, publishing, paper and insurance.

From the 1920s onwards, Birla increasingly played the role of spokesperson of Indian big business. A protagonist of solidarity among Indian businessmen, he helped establish the Indian Chamber of Commerce in Calcutta in 1925 and, later, FICCI in 1927. Both organizations were often controlled by factions close to him. Alongside, he carefully nurtured his networks with fellow Marwaris in Calcutta and Bombay, and was regarded as an elder whose counsel was sought often. In 1921, at the age of twenty-seven, Birla was nominated to the Bengal legislative council to represent Marwari commercial interests. He soon became a known figure within official circles and also developed close personal connections with a range of nationalist political leaders.

Through the 1910s and 1920s, he and his brothers had been strong financial supporters of Hindu nationalist leaders such as Madan Mohan Malaviya and Lala Lajpat Rai. From benefactor and financier, Birla soon became a colleague in the cause of Hindu nationalism, and in 1926, fought elections to the central legislative assembly on the ticket of the Independent Congress Party. His years in the assembly 'gave him a ring-side view of political life'. But by the end of his term, he decided to distance himself from active politics and to remain on the sidelines, as it were. Thereafter, he preferred the role of spokesperson of an influential section of Indian big business and, whenever necessary, was an emissary and mediator between the Indian political leadership and the British.

Birla also forged a close personal relationship with Gandhi and became an important financier of the 'constructive' causes that the Mahatma espoused. In 1932, he became the founding president of the All India Harijan Sevak Sangh, Gandhi's favourite constructive programme. Always careful to distinguish between his almost familial relation with the Mahatma and his political allegiance to him, Birla liked to call himself a 'Gandhi man'.

Not unexpectedly, Birla, like Thakurdas, had lukewarm relations with Jawaharlal Nehru, who envisaged a predominant role for the state in economic life. While distancing himself from Nehru's economic philosophy, Birla was astute enough not to openly take a stand against him but to work through other leaders who also opposed Nehru's radicalism. Thus, in 1936, when many of his peers were at odds with Nehru, he advised them against any action. Though he shared their concerns, he did not want an open, public attack on the Congress president. He was surprised that Thakurdas, despite being 'such a cautious man', could sign a manifesto against Nehru which, he told his friend, would merely give 'impetus to the forces working against capitalism'. To Birla, this was short-sighted and sounded 'very crude for a man of property to say that he is opposed to expropriation in the wider context of the country'.[25] Behind this stance lay Birla's conviction that the interests of private enterprise could best be served through centrist parties like the Congress. (Birla's nuanced approach was later evident in the 1950s and 1960s too—*see Chapter 7*—during the general business disquiet with Nehruvian socialism.)

Since the 1930s, Birla had become especially close to Vallabhbhai Patel and to a range of Congress leaders such as Rajendra Prasad and C. Rajagopalachari—the so-called 'right-wing' group within the Congress, many of whom were frequent guests at Birla's residences. Patel often sought Birla's advice on economic matters, and the two men shared similar views on many important issues.[26] Since the outbreak of the War, Birla had played the role of negotiator between Gandhi and the British, but relations between him and Viceroy Linlithgow had become somewhat strained as Birla was suspected of financing Gandhi's movements. In 1942, Birla, like Thakurdas, tried hard to dissuade Gandhi from launching the 'Quit India' movement, even though

Gandhi was staying at his home in Bombay and it was the venue for many important discussions in the lead-up to the 'Quit India' resolution. Interestingly, Gandhi was finally arrested from Birla's house.

Birla's closest friend in the group was the forty-eight-year-old Kasturbhai Lalbhai. Prominent in public life for at least two decades, Kasturbhai's involvement with business organizations dated back to 1918 when he became a member of the managing committee of the Ahmedabad Mill-Owners Association (the 'Manchester of India', Ahmedabad was second only to Bombay in the textile industry). Kasturbhai later held the positions of vice president from 1923 to 1936 and president in 1936–37. At the national level, he had been an active member of the Indian Currency League and of FICCI (where he was president in 1934). He had also been a member of the central legislative assembly in 1924, at the same time as Birla and Thakurdas as a representative of the Ahmedabad Mill-Owners Association, with the support of Vallabhbhai Patel. Some of his later important positions were as delegate to the International Labour Conference in Geneva in 1929; unofficial adviser to the government during the Indo-British Trade Negotiations in 1936–38; adviser to the Indian team for the Indo-Burma Trade agreement in 1940; and, perhaps most prestigious of all, director of the Reserve Bank of India since 1937.[27]

Kasturbhai belonged to a leading Oswal Jain merchant family, which had a hereditary claim to the title of Nagarseth, a 'principal man' or 'leader' among Hindus and

Jains, of Ahmedabad. When his father died suddenly in 1912, Kasturbhai, then seventeen, took over the family's small Raipur Mill. The wartime demand for cotton during 1914–18 and the challenges of the fluctuating market during the interwar period taught him to follow a cautious strategy of small initial investments, high reserves and modest dividends while valuing innovation in management and marketing. Cast in the traditional Jain mould, he valued kinship connections and the joint family network, whose interests played an important role in the decisions he took. He preferred the traditional managing agency system that allowed him to maintain family control, though he ensured professionalization in management. Concern for quality, fair play in business, and integrity, as his biographer Dwijendra Tripathi points out, were more important to him than outright expansion.

By 1927, he had brought one of the old mills out of liquidation. Between 1928 and 1931, he added three more mills and, in 1935, he bought another. Kasturbhai was one of the few Indian industrialists who expanded his business during the years of the Great Depression by taking advantage of the lower prices of machinery. In 1939, he started diversifying into chemicals, with plans for entering starch manufacture.

Like many other businesspersons, Kasturbhai's politics was driven by his concerns about the Indian economy. While he was a member of the central legislative assembly, Kasturbhai worked closely with leaders like Motilal Nehru and Vithalbhai Patel. Although Kasturbhai did not join any political party, he attended most meetings of the Swaraj Party, prompting Motilal to view him as a better Swarajist than regular party members.[28] Kasturbhai grew close to Gandhi during the 1910s and 1920s, though he too, like Birla, did not support Gandhi's agitational style of politics. Like his fellow Ahmedabad industrialists, Kasturbhai came under Gandhi's influence soon after the Mahatma took up residence at Sabarmati Ashram on his return to India from South Africa in 1915. He met Gandhi frequently, attended his prayer meetings and grew to deeply respect the Mahatma. Gandhi had the persona of a guru, and Kasturbhai, like his friend Birla, was charmed by the Mahatma and developed a quasi-religious, quasi-filial relationship with him.[29] Gandhi's austere lifestyle resounded in Kasturbhai's own lifestyle and in his insistence on limiting his personal needs.[30]

This did not mean that Kasturbhai agreed with Gandhi on political issues or necessarily supported all his political stances. An early occasion when they had differences was soon after Gandhi came to live in the Sabarmati Ashram and intervened in a workers' strike for continuance of a wartime plague bonus. Kasturbhai, like other Ahmedabad mill owners, felt the bonus wasn't necessary any longer since the plague epidemic was under control. Gandhi, however, intervened in support of the workers, going on a fast to persuade the mill owners to reach an amicable settlement with them. Kasturbhai viewed this as a coercive measure and castigated the Mahatma for meddling in an industrial dispute.[31] Yet he also empathized with the nationalist cause and was present at public protests in 1916, hosted mill owners' meetings during the 1918 textile strike, visited Gandhi often and supported his constructive activities, especially the propagation of khadi, his anti-untouchability measures and attempts to foster Hindu–Muslim unity. Like other businesspersons, Kasturbhai mostly kept aloof from Gandhi's mode of politics. One rare occasion when he went along with him was in 1930 when, perhaps on the bidding of Vallabhbhai Patel, Kasturbhai agreed to act as the custodian of funds for a trust associated with Gandhi, from which families of the Dandi marchers were being supported.[32] He avoided getting caught by the authorities as he was tipped off by Shri Ram who called to warn him of an impending raid by the police.[33]

Kasturbhai too wasn't happy with the leftist stance of Jawaharlal Nehru, although the two men were related because of the marriage of Nehru's sister, Krishna, to Kasturbhai's nephew, Gunnottam Hutheesing, in 1933. In 1936, Kasturbhai did not sign the Bombay manifesto against Nehru, possibly due to the familial connection and the influence of Birla, though it was widely rumoured that he had been one of those who had encouraged Shroff and his Bombay colleagues to put together the manifesto in the first instance.[34]

By 1942, Kasturbhai was one of the biggest textile magnates in the subcontinent, with seven mills that together contained 2,35,060 spindles, 11,425 looms and employed 12 per cent of Ahmedabad's labour force.[35] He had diversified into the manufacture of starch and sulphuric acid, and was in talks with American Cyanamid about producing synthetic dyestuffs and pharmaceuticals when World War II broke out. Yet, he remained conservative in his investment, deliberately limiting himself to western India in his business interests. In early August 1942, he visited Bombay when the decision to start the 'Quit India' movement was being taken. He returned to Ahmedabad the night before Gandhi announced its launch and happened to meet Khandubhai Desai, president of Ahmedabad's Textile Labour Association, on the overnight train home. Kasturbhai agreed to support a strike in support of the nationalist movement—a strike that was still under way when the seven men met in December 1942.

The only businessman from north India in the group was Lala Shri Ram. Although he had recently received a knighthood in 1941, he was perhaps the least well known of the group outside north Indian commercial circles. It was only in the last ten years that Shri Ram was beginning to emerge on the national scene, both in terms of his business ventures and his public persona. Till the 1930s, his main organizational link was with the Delhi Hindustan Mercantile Association, a body of cloth traders mainly from Delhi, headquartered in Chandni Chowk, of which he had also been president. In 1929, with the support of Thakurdas, he had become vice president of FICCI and the following year was elected its president. Shri Ram was known for his support to technical and commercial education: a high school which he had set up in the early 1920s had been converted into a college of commerce in 1926 with affiliation to the University of Delhi.

Shri Ram belonged to a conservative Bania family from Hissar, which had settled in Delhi in the nineteenth century. His uncle and father were both secretaries in Delhi Cloth and General Mills (later renamed DCM), which was founded in 1888. Shri Ram joined DCM in 1909 as assistant to his father. Though an old banking family, they were bankers 'more by repute than by occupation' till war profits brought them industrial fame.[36] During the years before World War I, DCM was in a downward spiral, with its output shrinking, profits falling and its shares selling at half their face value. War changed all this. Government orders for army tents and related supplies led to a rise in sales, and the firm earned its highest profits in 1917 after 1905. Most of the profit was made by selling tents, both for war purposes as well as for civil servants whose offices had been shifted from Calcutta to the new capital, New Delhi.

Personally, the war profits enabled Shri Ram and his father, both secretaries of the company till then, to gain control over DCM by increasing their holdings to 16 per cent. Most significantly, DCM, led by Shri Ram, switched over from yarn production to cloth during World War I. And once in charge, Shri Ram extended DCM's interests by adding new mills, including the Lyallpur Cotton Mills. Shri Ram and his father also set up two sugar mills, and DCM acquired a majority share in Bengal Potteries, a ceramics enterprise. In 1937, DCM ventured into the light engineering sector with the takeover of the Calcutta-based Jay Engineering Works, which became India's first precision light engineering enterprise with a complementary marketing and service network.

Shri Ram was not as involved with public affairs or particularly close to any nationalist leaders or British officials as the others in the group. He was still mainly a Delhi player, slowly gaining prominence because of his association with FICCI. Perhaps the most testing time for him politically was during his term as FICCI president in 1930, which coincided with the launch of Gandhi's Civil Disobedience movement. FICCI was divided over the issue of participation in the First Round Table Conference. Shri Ram himself favoured participation in the conference but was persuaded to support the move to boycott it. He urged Congress to consult with FICCI before taking any economic decisions and asked Gandhi to take steps to develop 'a sort of convention for the future that in all matters pertaining to the realm of economics, the Congress before making up its mind will allow us to offer it our suggestions and if necessary have discussion'.[37]

The outbreak of World War II coincided with the lavish golden jubilee celebrations of DCM. Shri Ram personally handed out to his employees 2000 Swiss watches that he had bought during a recent trip to Europe.[38] These were once again years of enormous profits because of the surge in war-related production. The cotton mills were operating round the clock, producing ready-made garments, tents and durries, while the sugar mills were earning huge profits after Japanese supplies were cut off, Bengal Potteries began to produce crockery for government orders, and Jay Engineering also switched to production of goods for the war effort. Little is known of Shri Ram's political allegiances, but it is telling that at the height of World War II, he accepted the offer of knighthood by the British— something his son, Bharat Ram, vehemently disapproved of.[39] His biographers confess he 'eagerly sought honours' from the British.[40]

The economists

JRD persuaded two economists associated with the Tata group, A.D. Shroff and John Matthai, to attend the meeting at Bombay House. The third economist, Lokanathan, was roped in at a later stage by Birla.

The highly articulate forty-three-year-old Shroff was a well-known figure in west India. Having played an active part in a number of commercial organizations over the last two decades, Shroff was specially reputed for his financial expertise, and his views were taken seriously in official circles. In 1936, Sir Osborne Smith, the first governor of the Reserve Bank of India, had even proposed that Shroff be appointed deputy governor, but the suggestion was turned down because he was seen to be a 'Congress economist'.[41]

Shroff had come a long way from his rather humble Parsi background. His father, Darabshaw Shroff, had worked for the cotton purchasing department of Killick Nixon. Shroff was the first graduate in the family, with a degree in history and economics from Bombay's Elphinstone College, also Thakurdas's alma mater. He then did a BSc from LSE with banking and currency as his special subjects. His tuition fees were defrayed by his earnings as an intern at a small bank—the Equitable Trust Company of New York—a position he secured on the recommendation of R.D. Tata. On his return to Bombay, again with the help of R.D. Tata, he landed a job with Batlivala & Karani, then the biggest brokerage firm, which was the house broker for Tata Sons. Like other brokers at that time, Batlivala & Karani floated initial public offerings of firms and also risked underwriting the issues.[42] They were responsible for floating the blue-chip Tata issues. Alongside, Shroff taught a banking class at Sydenham College of Commerce and Economics. He spent a good fifteen years at Batlivala & Karani, a most 'exciting' time for him. As a broker, he honed his skills in investment analyses of stocks traded in Bombay, London and New York, and in studying general market trends. Soon, the city's commercial circles began regarding Shroff as a 'financial wizard', and he became well known for his 'prodigious memory . . . particularly for figures'. It was rumoured that he could narrate—verbatim—the entire portfolios of at least 250 clients!

Shroff began to take an interest in Bombay's commercial life and became an active participant in the Bombay Shareholders Association, the Indian Merchants Chamber, the Indian Currency League and a number of other commercial organizations. From the 1920s, his main concern—much like that of Thakurdas—was the government's financial administration.[43] The two men worked closely together in the Indian Merchants Chamber's Committee and the Indian Currency League. Shroff's financial expertise led him to be elected chairman of the Bombay Municipal Finance Committee and to be invited to a number of official positions, such as member of the select committee of the Central Legislative Assembly when it was examining the Reserve Bank Bill in 1934.

Shroff's political inclinations were similar to those of his Bombay friends, especially his bosses in the Tata group. He was a die-hard constitutionalist, wedded to liberal methods and opposed to the ways of the Gandhi-led Indian National Congress.[44] Agitational politics, he believed, would harm the economic situation, especially in view of the trade depression that the country was witnessing.[45] Shroff found the attention given to political issues tiresome and believed that economic and financial matters needed much more consideration.

However, by the late 1920s, the resistance of the colonial state to amend its financial policy, especially the sterling-rupee ratio, persuaded him to modify his apolitical stance and grow more sympathetic to the methods of the Mahatma.[46] Along with his peers in Bombay, in January 1930 he supported the eleven-point memorandum of demands put forth by Gandhi to the Viceroy, which included reduction of the sterling-rupee ratio and other commercial demands, such as protective tariff against foreign imports. Shroff believed the Mahatma had been 'inspired by the bitter experience of Indians that the country's public finances have not been administered in the interest of India.'[47]

Much like his fellow businessmen in the 1930s, Shroff was deeply sceptical about Nehru's political leanings and his advocacy of 'socialism', especially as he grew more important in the Congress hierarchy and became party president in 1936.[48] That year, Shroff was vice president of both the Indian Merchants Chamber, the biggest commercial body in western India, and of the Bombay Shareholders Association. With characteristic candour, Shroff condemned Nehru's ideas as 'more likely to injure the best interest of this country by curbing industrial enterprise and encouraging flight of capital from India'.[49] Shroff galvanized twenty-one of the most influential people in Bombay's commercial community, including almost the entire board of Tata Sons and Thakurdas, to put together a manifesto critiquing Nehru's socialist views.[50]

Later, in 1938, Shroff was invited to be a member of the Congress's National Planning Committee. In 1940, he left Batlivala & Karani to become full-time director with the Tatas, serving mainly as their financial advisor with the charge of setting up the Investment Corporation of India.[51] After the outbreak of the War, he was busy with the group's stock market operations and organization of its fund collection for the War Gift Fund proposed by the governor.[52]

The other in-house economist roped in by JRD was Dr John Matthai, a recently appointed director of Tata

Sons, who formulated many of the early ideas that finally evolved into the Bombay Plan. Matthai belonged to a Syrian orthodox Jacobite family from Kottayam. After a bachelor's in history from Madras Christian College, in which he secured a 'first class' in 1905, he was immediately offered a tutorship in the history department, which he held till 1908. Interested in history, law and economics, Matthai began to study law at Madras Law College and started practice as a lawyer at the Madras High Court. Deeply involved with church activity, he gave up law in 1912 under the influence of evangelists, according to his biographer, when he was defending an accused in a murder case and had to coach witnesses to present a false defence. Matthai then joined the Madras YMCA as assistant general secretary. Interested in pursuing a doctorate, he tried for a scholarship from the Tatas but had to finally pay for his education himself, and in 1913 joined LSE for a DSc degree. He paid his fees by teaching at a Sunday school in London and working part-time at the India Office. For his doctorate, Matthai analysed village governance in British India and worked with the famous Fabian, Sydney Webb. Thereafter, he went to Balliol College, Oxford, for a BLitt in 1917.

On his return to India, Matthai secured a position as assistant registrar of cooperative societies in the cooperative department of the Madras Presidency. He soon came to be noticed for his grasp of financial issues, and in 1922 was nominated by Lord Wellingdon to the Madras legislative council where he served two terms. Alongside, he taught economics at Madras University from 1922 to 1925 and was active in economic debates by participating in the annual Indian Economic Conference. He was selected as a member of the Indian Tariff Board in 1925 and later became its president from 1931 to 1934. Between 1935 and 1940, he was director general of commercial intelligence and statistics. In 1940, he joined Tata Sons as vice chairman of Tata Steel and was later given the specific charge of Tata Chemicals. Matthai was well known for his eloquence and hard-hitting humour, combined with a serene personality.[53]

The third economist who worked on the Bombay Plan, although he was not a signatory, was P.S. Lokanathan, a Birla employee. Lokanathan's first degree was from St Joseph's College, Trichinopoly, and he did his master's in economics from the University of Madras. These were formative years for Lokanathan, when he came under the influence of teachers such as John Matthai, then recently back from England, Gilbert Slater, an important Fabian, and T.K. Duraiswami Aiyar who specialized in indigenous banking. After his graduation, Lokanathan worked as a research assistant for Slater, helping him collect material on the economic conditions of the village people in the Tirunelveli district.[54] Lokanathan was then appointed reader at Madras University in 1927. During these years, he wrote on industrial welfare, and his first major work, *Industrial Welfare in India*, was published by the University of Madras in 1929. Given his initiation in economics under Matthai and Slater, it is not surprising that Lokanathan too decided to pursue his doctorate from LSE too. There he worked on industrial organization in India, the development of large-scale industry and the managing agency system. In 1935, he published *Industrial Organization in India*, which soon came to be recognized as a classic. On his return from London, Lokanathan rejoined the University of Madras. His work earned him a place on important committees in the state, such as the Labour Advisory Board of the Government of Madras. Lokanathan was known to be deeply sensitive to inequity and, as a younger colleague of his recalled, he 'was probably the only economist who has gone on record to say that the entire gains of productivity should in the first instance be devoted to raising wages to a minimum wage level'.[55] In 1942, he was invited by Devdas Gandhi to Delhi to assist him with the forthcoming Birla publication, the *Eastern Economist*, and soon became its editor.

A man for all seasons

The ninth member of the group was Ardeshir Dalal who, along with Lokanathan, was roped in later. However, Dalal, unlike Lokanathan, was a signatory to the Bombay Plan, even though he was not present at the 11 December meeting. But Dalal was signatory only to Part I of the Plan, published in January 1944, since he was co-opted by the government to be its member-in-charge of planning before the publication of Part II in December 1944.

Like JRD and Shroff, Dalal was a Parsi. His father, Rustomji Dalal, was a broker at the Bombay Stock Exchange. Ardeshir got his first degree from Elphinstone College. He then did a tripos in natural science from St John's College, Cambridge, where he was the recipient of the J.N. Tata scholarship. On his return to India, he secured the second position in the Indian Civil Service exam in 1908. Like all civil servants, Dalal had to serve in different positions. Among the posts he held were secretary to the Government of Bombay in the finance department, secretary to the Government of India in education, health and lands, and from 1928 onwards, municipal commissioner of Bombay. He gained high acclaim as municipal commissioner when he effected a reorganization of various departments that led to an annual savings of nearly Rs 6 lakh in establishment charges. He was also much admired for his effective handling of successive outbreaks of malaria. Recognized for his grasp of financial matters, Dalal was regarded as one of the ablest commissioners of Bombay. After retiring from government service in 1931, he joined the Tatas as resident director of the Tata Iron and Steel Company. He was soon appointed on the boards of various Tata companies and began to work on introducing a profit-sharing bonus scheme in the company. Dalal fitted the role well. 'Extremely well-groomed', he was known for his 'indefinable atmosphere of preciseness' but also for his volatile temper in Bombay House. In 1939, he received a knighthood and, during the War, was appointed as liaison officer in 1941 for the ministry of supplies with specific responsibility for iron and steel control.

A meeting of minds

Together, these nine men wielded enormous clout in India's commercial and political circles. For more than three decades, many of them had held leadership positions in commercial organizations across India, and five had been key players in the foremost commercial organization, FICCI. All of them enjoyed considerable access and influence in official circles too. JRD, Thakurdas, Birla, Kasturbhai, Shri Ram, Dalal and Shroff shared cordial relations with British officials at the apex level.[56] Three held knighthoods (Thakurdas, Dalal and Shri Ram), while Birla had refused the honour. Three (Thakurdas, Kasturbhai and Shri Ram) were directors of the Reserve Bank of India and many of them sat on official committees on financial and economic matters.

Simultaneously, they had nurtured relations with prominent nationalist leaders across the spectrum. Birla and Kasturbhai were especially close to Gandhi and Vallabhbhai Patel. Birla was often sought by the Congress leadership, especially Patel, for advice on economic issues, such as the budget and the sterling question. Shroff's advice too was sought by Gandhi on financial matters.[57] Kasturbhai shared a familial relationship with Nehru, and JRD, like the other Tatas, had an old friendship with the Nehru family. Thakurdas and Shroff had been members of the national planning committee of the Congress since 1938 and had close relations with many leaders, even though they did not always agree with or support their political views.

Between them, at least six shared working relationships of more than two decades, from the late 1910s to the 1920s, when they came together on the currency issue. They had, through these long years, often differed in their opinions and political views, yet had found a way of putting aside their disagreements to work together on what they saw as the need of the hour. This time too, they joined hands in the larger cause.

Since the outbreak of World War II, even as members of the group faced similar challenges and saw common opportunities, there was a change in their old relationships and a new willingness to work together for the common good. Much of this had to do with business's belied expectations and the consequent disillusionment with the colonial regime during the war years. As we have seen in Chapter 1, with hopes of an 'industrial renaissance' receding, disenchantment with official policies deepened, and the widely accepted view was that, through the War, 'India's vital economic interests have been [were] subordinated to those of Britain's economic interests.' Businesspersons were coming around to the view that a 'national government is . . . essential not only for war effort but also for safeguarding India's economic and financial interests'.[58] Unsurprisingly then, all nine architects of what came to be known as the Bombay Plan were willing to come together and work towards formulating some sort of plan for the post-war economy.

There was also, significantly, a closing of ranks with the nationalists during this period. Earlier, big business had disapproved of the decision taken by the Congress in 1939 to resign from all the provincial governments, since businesspersons had achieved a certain level of stability in their relations with the Congress during its term in government.[59] Even the subsequent Civil Disobedience and 'Quit India' movements launched by Gandhi were not welcomed by business. Thakurdas, Kasturbhai and Birla, in particular, attempted a reconciliation between the Congress and the government in the days leading up to the movement.[60] Some were trying till even 8 August 1942 to persuade Gandhi, who was staying at Birla House, to change his mind before the All India Congress Committee formally adopted the 'Quit India' resolution a day later. There was much disappointment that Gandhi was unmoved by their exhortations. Lamenting the Mahatma's action, Thakurdas wrote to Birla: '. . . what Indian nationalism had built up during the last thirty years has been ruined, at least for the time being . . . Could there be a more pathetic setback to the efforts of the Congress than this?'[61]

Despite their discontent with this turn of events, they rallied in support of the nationalist cause after the repression unleashed by the colonial government. Birla, JRD, Thakurdas, and Kasturbhai, along with other peers, appealed to the viceroy: 'We are all businessmen and, therefore, need hardly point out that our interest lies in

peace, harmony, goodwill and order throughout the country . . . We submit that the need of the hour is not strong action, but a proper and sympathetic understanding and tactful handling of a grave situation.'[62] Numerous political issues were now taken up by them in their individual capacities and, at a collective level, by their regional commercial organizations and FICCI. Some of the matters raised included the severe repression unleashed by the colonial government, the release of Indian political leaders who had been imprisoned, the denial of a meeting between C. Rajagopalachari and Gandhi in jail, and the mission led by Stafford Cripps to foster reconciliation. Once these mediatory efforts were rebuffed by the British, there was no turning back for the business leaders. It was this meeting of minds which brought the nine men together to think through what the post-war future could hold for the Indian economy.

4

THE INTELLECTUAL
CONTEXT OF THE PLAN

Held during the troubled years of World War II, the meeting at Bombay House on 11 December 1942 was convened against the backdrop of fierce intellectual debate among economists the world over about post-war reconstruction. Problems plaguing the global economy since the Great Depression in the 1930s and the resulting widespread hardships had been the subject of intense deliberations. Was it socialism or capitalism that offered a more efficient economic system? Could they coexist or would they inevitably clash? How could market fluctuations and unemployment be reined in?

Though there were a number of different views and opinions, by the early 1940s it was clear that the main ideological battle was being fought in economic circles in Britain. One group was led by Friedrich August von

Hayek, the leading scholar of the 'Austrian' school, and the other group by John Maynard Keynes, the celebrated Cambridge economist, civil servant and lead adviser during the Paris Peace talks of 1919. The debate between these two camps was to have a lasting impact on the post-war economic policies followed by different countries. Not surprisingly, the issues in contention also deeply influenced the discussions at Bombay House and so need to be briefly outlined.

Hayek versus Keynes

Hayek had been a gunner during World War I, then went on to finish two doctorates at the University of Vienna. On the eve of the Great Depression he had moved to LSE, securing a faculty position (Tooke Chair of Economic Science and Statistics) where he created something of a stir with his insightful lectures on the causes of economic booms and busts. Rumour had it that he had been called to LSE to 'provide a counter-attraction' to Keynes at Cambridge.[1] The erudite Hayek soon became LSE's star theorist, a 'major stimulus to thought', and took over the editorship of its prestigious journal, *Economica*.[2]

The personal experiences of Hayek and Keynes during World War I and in the years thereafter led them to radically different conclusions about the wisdom of allowing free-market capitalism to run its course. Keynes's stint as a policymaker having to deal with appallingly high levels of unemployment in Britain during the 1920s led him to support public spending, while Hayek's service as a gunner in the War, the devastation of his beloved Vienna, and the post-war hardships inflicted on Austria made him very sceptical of public spending and instilled in him a fear of inflation.

The two men were engaged in a prolonged intellectual duel over the desirability of state-funded programmes and whether private investment in the public sphere was the best route to creating general wealth and prosperity. The Keynes–Hayek debate went through many rounds, starting with capital deflation versus demand management, business-cycle theory and monetary overinvestment of the trade cycle, international trade, and then extending to the wider problem of the functioning of the market economy.[3] Keynes's understanding of the Great Depression led him to believe that the market could not be trusted to provide full employment. He thus countered the classical view that markets are 'fundamentally stable and will tend to move the economy toward equilibrium at the highest practicable rate of employment'.[4] To him, some form of state intervention was necessary to tame the market. Keynes thus advocated state intervention in demand management, resource mobilization for development and investment, and the use of public expenditure to avoid cyclical unemployment. He attacked the priority which classical economists attached to a balanced budget and did not want fiscal constraints to stand in the way of generous social programmes. He asked governments to increase their own expenditure (or to lower taxes) as this injection of funds would increase the aggregate purchasing power of consumers by a multiple of the original amount, with funds passing from one hand to another through various transactions.[5] Keynes's three main prescriptions to deal with the Great Depression were maintenance of low interest rates through central control; redistribution of wealth through taxation to increase the propensity to consume; and increasing government spending to augment insufficient private investment.

While Keynes advocated active policy responses by the state, Hayek, on the other hand, desired non-interventionism and free trade. Hayek was a critic of collectivism, on the moral ground that it did not encourage freedom of thought.[6] A sceptic of big governments, Hayek viewed the market economy in terms of its successful allocation of resources through the decentralized decisions of buyers and sellers, and the 'spontaneous order' this brought as a superior system to planned economies. He took a liberal view of the proper functioning of the state, which 'should make as much use as possible of the spontaneous forces of society and resort as little as possible to coercion'. He believed that large-scale public spending along Keynesian lines would lead to uncontrollable inflation and, worse still, political turmoil. Liberty and personal responsibility were ends in themselves and 'could not be bartered away to add to the sum total of economic satisfaction'. For these reasons, Hayek condemned central planning or a central direction of economic activity according to a single plan.[7] He feared total planning with centralized control; a planning which subverted individual freedom.

Yet Hayek was not advocating laissez faire: he was in favour of a minimum income for everyone, a comprehensive social security organization, actively combating general fluctuations in the economy as well as large-scale unemployment. As such, Hayek was not against planning, but condemned 'planning against competition— the planning which is a substitute for competition'. In his view, competition was not incompatible with systems of social security; he was against monopoly and pushed for real competition.[8]

Despite their clear divergence of views on most matters, there was some measure of common ground between Keynes and Hayek. Both economists, like so many of their peers, had been influenced by the violent market fluctuations of the Great Depression of the 1930s. Both shared a loss of faith in market mechanisms, and both were also convinced that economic order needed some state intervention. In the prevailing dismal atmosphere of the time, 'most economists' aspired to, as Arthur Cecil Pigou, professor of political economy, a contemporary and rival of Keynes at King's College, Cambridge, put it so aptly, 'help in some degree, directly or indirectly towards social betterment'.[9] Pigou's own engagement had been with understanding problems of unequal distribution of wealth and social welfare, and to find ways to diminish inequalities.[10] Many economists in the pre-war period felt there needed to be some sort of 'purposive direction by the state' in order to 'preserve regularity in the economic system to avoid the hideous alternation of boom and slump'. However, no consensus seemed to exist on what this would entail.[11] Both Hayek and Keynes were against authoritarian regimes and were trying to hold on to a liberal, democratic stance while also recognizing that capitalism could not be allowed to operate without any moral constraints whatsoever.

Even till the late 1930s, it was by no means clear that Keynes would come to have the upper hand against Hayek. Keynes's landmark book, *The General Theory of Employment, Interest and Money*, published in 1936, appeared then to be just another addition to the polemic, even though it called for entirely new ways of looking at how gross national product was determined and was seen in hindsight to mark the advent of the new field of macroeconomics.[12] Hayek's influential libertarian classic, *The Road to Serfdom*, on the other hand, appeared only later in 1944, in which he argued that extensive planning was not only incapable of promoting general prosperity but also posed a grave threat to basic liberties.[13]

What won the day for Keynesianism was the outbreak of World War II, the after-effects of which had a profound effect on the study of economics. Keynes's diagnosis of the Great Depression as a massive failure of aggregate demand appeared to be validated when war-induced demand finally succeeded in ending the Depression. The War itself had been financed through massive borrowings by the different countries involved. This led nations to accept the legitimacy of deliberate state intervention to boost the economy. By the end of the War, mainstream macroeconomics became predominantly Keynesian, as his *General Theory* succeeded in collapsing the rich debates of the interwar years into a 'static, short-run, aggregate model concerned exclusively with a closed economy'.[14] A 'Keynesian avalanche' occurred, from which few economists could escape.[15] In Britain, for instance, William Beveridge's ideas on full employment, and in the United States, the Employment Act of 1946 became blueprints for state intervention in the economy along Keynesian lines. Keynes's ideas increasingly provided the foundation upon which many nations built their systems of macroeconomic management in the post-war era.[16]

Echoes of the Keynes–Hayek debate in India

A frontline witness to the Keynes–Hayek debate in London was Lokanathan, who had arrived at LSE as a student two years before Hayek joined LSE. Though Lokanathan and his peers must certainly have engaged with the ideas of Hayek and his strident critique of 'Cambridge economics', they were getting swayed by Keynes's theories, which appeared to present an economic vision 'more closely attuned to the circumstances of the 1930s'.[17] LSE 'did not know how to react to the evident ascendancy of Cambridge' and, notwithstanding the 'Keynesian revolution', continued to cling on to its older approach.[18] So fierce was the institutional opposition to Keynes that, on one occasion, when LSE students invited him for a talk, they were allotted only a small room on the fourth floor of the school's building for the event. This, however, did not deter the crowds, and many were happy to listen to Keynes from outside the room.[19]

Keynes's ideas resonated with Lokanathan, as well as with Matthai and Shroff, as they felt that in them lay the answers to all the problems of India. The Keynesian prescriptions in terms of demand management and public spending greatly impressed them, and this found a place in the text of the Bombay Plan. Later, however, when Hayek's book was published in 1944, they took cognizance of his warnings and included them in Masani's popular edition of the Plan which was printed in 1945.

The three economists apart, the other authors of the Bombay Plan were also familiar with Keynes's ideas. The engagement of Indian business leaders with Keynes went back at least twenty years to 1911, when Keynes published his tract, *Indian Currency and Finance*. In this work, Keynes put forth a strong defence of the gold-exchange standard being most suitable for India, rather than the traditional gold standard. This meant that currency would be maintained at a fixed value against gold by way of sterling credits held in London. Countering the classical understanding of the gold standard, Keynes argued that the gold-exchange standard economized on the use of gold and made money more elastic to the actual needs of business. In his view, those who insisted that a reserve currency take the form of a physical commodity (gold) were misguided in backing a 'relic of a time when governments were less trustworthy in these matters than they are now'.[20] This ran completely counter to the long-standing arguments made by Bombay industrialists, especially the Bombay Mill-Owners Association, which, since the 1890s, had been asking for the Indian rupee to be linked to the gold standard. Indian industrialists had wanted a full gold standard with circulating gold coins, a promise made in 1893, as it was believed that gold inflow and outflow would then depend on India's balance of trade and thus adjustment of money supply would be automatic. In this way, it was felt, control of monetary policy would not be with the India Office. Indian economists like S.V. Doraiswamy supported this view and opposed Keynes. It was also believed that a gold standard would bring gold out of hoarding, thus solving the problem of scarcity of money.

The main concern of Indian industry was that the gold standard would prevent the colonial government from manipulating the rupee–sterling ratio. What made matters more urgent was that the value of the rupee—a silver coin—had risen to two shillings at the end of World War I. The increasing price of silver made the exchange rate effectively 2s 10d, a rate supported by officialdom. Indian businessmen, led by Thakurdas and later Shroff, opposed this high value of the rupee because it benefited British exporters selling to India and hurt Indian exports. So well articulated was their critique that it became almost an emotive issue, and almost all of the country's economic ills came to be blamed on the 'high ratio' adopted after the War. A concerted agitation on this was started by the businessmen in the early 1920s, led mainly by Thakurdas, with the help of experts such as the Parsi mill owner and close Tata associate, B.F. Madon, the economists C.N. Vakil and K.T. Shah of Bombay University and, later, A.D. Shroff.[21] Though Keynes was most famous for his advocacy of the use of fiscal and monetary policies by governments to shore up aggregate demand and prevent high unemployment, in India it was his views on the sterling–rupee ratio that attracted the most attention.

An opportunity to raise these issues in person with Keynes came to Thakurdas in March 1926 when, as a member of the Hilton Young Royal Commission on Indian Finance, Currency and Practice, he met the famous economist who appeared as a witness before the commission. Keynes had submitted a written memorandum on the proposal for a gold standard for India, in which he argued that it would have no advantage 'except to placate Indian opinion', which would be 'misguided'.[22] Thakurdas grilled Keynes, sometimes in a terse tone, and asked as many as seventy questions. Keynes's memorandum, submitted earlier, had set out his views on the ideal currency for India, raised the question of regulating exchange rates, made the case for a central bank to be the note-issuing authority and stated his opinions on the sterling–rupee ratio.[23] Keynes's main contentions were that there was no advantage in having a gold currency over a gold-exchange standard, that a central bank be set up for better control of currency and that the issue of exchange rate should not 'overbear every other object'. The economist Anand Chandavarkar has argued that Keynes was personally sympathetic to the Indian point of view on the exchange question, but this could not have been apparent to Thakurdas then.[24] In keeping with the colonial view, the Hilton Young Commission supported an exchange rate of 1s 6d to the rupee on the ground that prices needed to be adjusted to world prices. This forced Thakurdas to write a note of dissent in favour of depreciating the exchange rate to 1s 4d. The interaction between Thakurdas and Keynes marked the beginning of an uneasy relationship between the Bombay Plan authors and the economist, which only worsened over the years over issues such as the sterling balance and the encounter between Shroff and Keynes at Bretton Woods in 1944.

The 'planning' idea

Even as late as 1933, the Oxford English Dictionary did not recognize the existence of the word 'planning'—a clear indicator that the idea of planning was still somewhat novel.[25] Gradually, however, during the interwar years, a more direct interventionist role for the state was accepted, and it got a further boost because of the sheer practical needs of the war effort. In Britain, the mobilization required for 'total war'—whether in terms of equipping the armed forces, running an efficient war economy or preventing hardships for the general public—led the state to intervene in almost all aspects of people's lives.[26] The assumptions of laissez faire liberalism stood challenged as it was shown what states could achieve once growth objectives had been clearly defined.

As a result of the war experience, many economists had come around to the need for planning. Planning was 'in the air', even though there was as yet no 'model' of planning. The only work that could be considered an early systematic treatment on planning was by Roy Harrod, the British economist and younger colleague of Keynes who was then at Christ Church College, Oxford. Harrod's 'An Essay in Dynamic Theory', published in March 1939 in the *Economic Journal*, spelt out conditions under which 'additions to productive capacity, generated by new investment, would be absorbed by the additional income likewise generated by the new investment'.[27] Harrod made the case that entrepreneurial goals were best served by seizing the largest market share, setting prices so low as to deter competition, avoiding overcapacity and, as a result, maximizing profits in the long run. However, other economic debates took centre stage and Harrod's model came to be neglected during the war years. It was, however, resurrected seven years later, in 1948, when Harrod, in collaboration with Evsey D. Domar, who was then at MIT, brought out the Harrod-Domar model. In simple terms, this predicted how much people must save and invest to keep the economy growing. The Harrod-Domar model became the buzzword in developmental planning till more sophisticated models emerged much later.

'The lure of a catching phrase'

Parallel to the overseas debate raging over planning, in India too the pre-war years saw heated arguments about what planning meant. There was no clarity on what its working or implementation would entail, and there were hotly contested debates on fundamental issues such as agriculture-led development versus industrialization, adoption of traditional technology and cottage industry versus modern technology and heavy industrialization, the socialist-versus-capitalist path, giving priority to consumer goods over capital goods and the means of raising finance for development programmes.[28]

By the mid-1930s, however, the necessity of state intervention in the economy had come to be generally accepted within Indian academic circles. The debate was not about whether there needed to be some kind of state intervention through planning but rather how much should take place. 'The unanimity of opinion on the subject of planning is as remarkable as it is impressive and if it is to be taken at its face value, it is an index to the growing desire of every section in India to join hands for the common good of all,' declared Gyanchand, the LSE-trained economist and a much respected professor, in 1935.[29] A key premise of this rather bold nationalist position was the call for state intervention in economic life, especially when it came to monetary policies such as the setting of exchange rates, tariff protection for indigenous production and reform of landholdings.

Amongst the advocates of planning, there were many different though overlapping intellectual strands that were being articulated. The extreme left view was represented in the *People's Plan for Economic Development of India*, authored by B.N. Banerjee, G.D. Parikh and V.M. Tarkunde in 1944 under the guidance of Manabendra Nath Roy, founder-member of the Communist International, an international communist body formed to advocate communism, and one time a trusted friend of no less a person than Lenin himself.[30] The *People's Plan*, published by the Indian Federation of Labour, emphasized agricultural development through mechanization, modernization and collectivization. The *People's Plan* also focused on hydroelectric power, mining and metallurgy, and iron and steel, besides consumer goods industries such as textiles, leather, sugar, paper, drugs and chemicals, tobacco, oil, furniture and glass. New industries were to be financed by the state and all privately owned enterprises placed under public control.[31]

The foremost proponent of those who pushed for planning with industrialization as a basis for national 'development' was Sir M. Visvesvaraya, engineer, civil servant and former dewan of Mysore. An ardent believer in the transformative capacity of science in the service of human development and a votary of large-scale industries, Visvesvaraya appealed to the colonial state in New Delhi to take active measures to promote industrialization which, he believed, would solve the dire problem of poverty in the country.

Then there was Jawaharlal Nehru, whose eclectic vision was shaped by his deep admiration of industrialization in the Soviet Union and his leanings towards Fabian socialism. The 1930s marked the apogee of Nehru's socialism, reflected both in his public speeches and in his writings, such as *Whither India* (1933). He called for a radical restructuring of the social and economic system, which would entail a structural transformation of the largely agrarian economy through land reforms, the formation of cooperatives, and industrialization, besides seeking equality for citizens, reduction in income disparities and in the concentration of economic power and, not the least, a key role for the public sector.[32]

Within the nationalist leadership, the most well-known sceptic of planning was none other than Mahatma Gandhi. His suspicion of planning stemmed from his ideas about the economic trajectory best suited to India, and it was an ethical standpoint rather than one based on any definitive system or fixed formulae.[33] For the Mahatma, ethical and economic considerations were inseparable in his larger vision to 'bring about improvements in both the economics and moral well-being of individuals and thereby of society'.[34] The basic premise of Gandhi's economic philosophy was the idea that an individual's welfare is best achieved by limiting wants. He envisaged self-reliant villages, sometimes termed as 'village republics', with a subsistence economy producing food and clothing, a dynamic agricultural sector and the spread of low-technology–based small-scale industries. For the rich, Gandhi contemplated a voluntary trusteeship role in which they would hold their wealth in trust for society in general. In his view, industrialization could not be the goal for India, although he did accept that some large-scale private industry would continue, especially in the production of cotton textiles, but trusteeship would ameliorate its ill effects. He opposed industrialization of agriculture through the adoption of large-scale mechanization, as this ran contrary to his ideal vision of an environmentally sustainable village-based society. Thus planning, which was predicated upon a centralized system of state control, was incompatible with Gandhi's vision.[35]

Gandhi was the odd man out because there was support for economic planning even among some official quarters. Most notably, Sir George Schuster, finance member of the viceroy's executive council, made efforts to set up an economic advisory council, consisting of officials as well as non-officials, with a view to steering policy that would give an increased role to the state in economic development.[36] Thus, individuals and agencies of widely divergent points of view and interests desired some sort of economic planning. This desire, contended Gyanchand, was 'due to our having fallen victim to the lure of a catching phrase'.[37]

5

THE PLAN ANALYSED

Thirteen months after the brainstorming session at Bombay House, *A Brief Memorandum Outlining a Plan of Economic Development for India*, or the Bombay Plan, as it was commonly known, was published on 17 January 1944.[1] Part II of the Plan, *Distribution—Role of the State*, was published later, in December 1944. The two parts of the ninety-page plan boldly declared a commitment to an independent nation, with the state playing a major role in economic development. Optimistic about India's economic future, the Plan envisaged two distinct phases of growth. In the first fifteen years, the trajectory was to be one of 'intensive planned development', during which the state's role would be significant, with widespread controls over production and distribution. Thereafter, a certain stage of economic development and a basic level of 'full employment' having been reached, the trajectory would change to follow 'normal times',[2] with the state's role being limited to macroeconomic decisions.

Before delving into any details, the authors enunciated the premises upon which the Plan was based. Foremost was the 'assumption' that a 'national government' would be formed at the end of the War. This would be vested with 'full freedom in economic matters'. A further 'essential condition' was economic unity in which the 'jurisdiction of the central government in economic matters' would extend over the whole of India.[3] While the Plan acknowledged that 'political factors have been tending towards fragmentation and partition', the authors believed that 'economic factors have been compelling in their effects and tend towards integration'.[4] India would need to be one economic entity in which the Centre's writ would run in all matters. No development could be possible, the planners pointed out, 'except on the basis of a central directing authority' with the necessary 'requisite powers and jurisdiction'. World War II had demonstrated the capacity of governments to mobilize productive forces and had convinced the planners about the need for a central coordinating authority.[5] Such thinking was bolstered by the Keynesian view of the need for vigorous state intervention in the markets.

A plan for prosperity: objectives and targets

The key objective of the Bombay Plan was to raise the standard of living and 'bring about a doubling of the per capita income within a period of fifteen years'. Driven by a desire to 'destroy poverty', 'one of the main purposes of the Plan', the ultimate goal was to achieve a minimum standard of living for the common man, which is regarded a fundamental right in an economic sense.[6] Thus, the Plan aimed at assuring to every person a minimum income essential for a 'reasonable standard of living'. It hoped that by the end of fifteen years the existing 'pyramid of wealth and income' would be 'replaced by an even surface'.[7] Eradicating mass poverty and lessening income inequality were both of central concern to the planners.

But it was not equality per se that was the ultimate objective; rather, the aim was that gross inequalities of income should be 'radically reduced'.[8] Not only did the planners acknowledge that achieving complete equality of income within fifteen years was impractical, but they also believed that it was not even desirable, nor in the 'interest of the country'.[9] For them, the 'incentive for efficiency' was crucial for building a sustainable economic structure. And such an incentive, they contended, could come only from within a capitalist framework. No shake-up of the economic order was envisaged; only reform was advised, because the existing order had 'failed to bring about a satisfactory distribution of national income'. Drawing support from Keynes's recently published *General Theory of Employment, Interest and Money*, the planners acknowledged that capitalism's features have 'stood the test of time' and have 'enduring achievements'. However, they desired free enterprise 'which is truly enterprising'. Ideally, what was expected from capitalism was a way of ensuring that the 'fruits of enterprise and labour are fairly apportioned among all those who contribute to them and not unjustly withheld by a few from the many'.[10] Citing Keynes, ('there is social and psychological justification for significant inequalities of incomes and wealth, but not for such large disparities as exist to-day'), they took the position that 'profit-seeking' is a harmless channel for 'dangerous human proclivities' which could otherwise 'find their outlet in cruelty, the reckless pursuit of personal power and authority, and other forms of self-aggrandizement'. 'The total abolition of inequalities was thus not desirable.' Instead, what was needed was a reduction of inequality—as a 'question of justice' since it was unfair, but also because 'gross inequality of income is uneconomic'.[11] The planners were conscious that poor domestic demand, due to the existing levels of inequality and poverty, could constrain growth. India's large population would also have no bearing on stimulating consumer demand because 'this unequal distribution of the national income also means that most of the people lack purchasing power . . . This means that there is little demand for goods and that production in its turn must be restricted . . .'[12] Thus, the Bombay Plan authors were concerned about boosting domestic demand. This was in contrast to the supply-side view of the economic problems in India their contemporaries subscribed to.

To increase domestic demand and reduce inequality, the Bombay Plan recommended a higher rate of growth that would lead to 'levelling up'[13] or a rise in the general level of income. Yet, this clearly would not suffice. The authors also thought about 'levelling down' measures to prevent overconsumption by the upper-income classes and thereby reduce disparities.[14] The main objective of the Bombay Plan was to achieve rapid and inclusive economic growth so that all individuals had the 'minimum requirements for human life'. These were defined in terms of essential needs—'the least amount of food, clothing or house space which a man requires'.[15] Besides these basic needs, the Plan stated, 'a person above the age of 10 should be able to read, write and take intelligent interest in private and social life', and this would constitute the 'minimum standard of living'.[16] The Plan thus defined its objective of ensuring that 'every individual would be left with enough resources for enjoyment of life and for cultural activities'.[17]

The first human need of roti was quantified at a daily 2800 calories per person.[18] At this calorific intake, India was barely producing five-sevenths of the food required in 1942.[19] There was a serious shortfall in *kapada* too. The minimum per capita requirement of cloth was calculated at thirty yards. This translated into an annual production requirement of 11,670 million yards for a population of 400 million.[20] To achieve this target, production needed to be doubled. Regarding *makaan,* the minimum accommodation was pegged at 100 sq feet per person. This called for a 'big building' programme of nearly 55,000,000 new houses, involving a capital expenditure of 6.6 billion dollars (Rs 1400 crore).[21]

The provision of potable water supply, sanitation and basic medical facilities—an estimated 700,000 doctors and 14,000,000 nurses[22] were required—was identified as another pressing need. Finally came education, which needed to be fortified at different levels, with the goal of eradicating illiteracy within fifteen years. The Plan proposed that both education and medical treatment should be free, while utility services such as electricity, gas and transport were to be minimally priced.

Based on these calculations, the Plan arrived at a basic income required to secure essential goods and services, and drew a per capita poverty line of Rs 74 at pre-war prices.[23] To achieve even this would require no less than a doubling of per capita income within fifteen years. The Plan laid down macro- and micro-level targets in various sectors that were envisaged to yield, over the fifteen-year interim period, a 130 per cent increase in agricultural output, a 500 per cent increase in industry, and a 200 per cent increase in services. This, in turn, meant that contributions by the three sectors of agriculture, industry and services to the national income would alter from their existing proportions of '53, 17, and 22 per cent, respectively, to 40, 35, and 20 per cent'.[24] The share of workforce in the different sectors would also change: agriculture would account for 58 per cent (down from 73 per cent), industry would absorb 26 per cent (increasing from 15 per cent in 1931), and employment in the services sector would rise marginally, from 13 per cent to approximately 16 per cent.[25]

The Plan and Agriculture

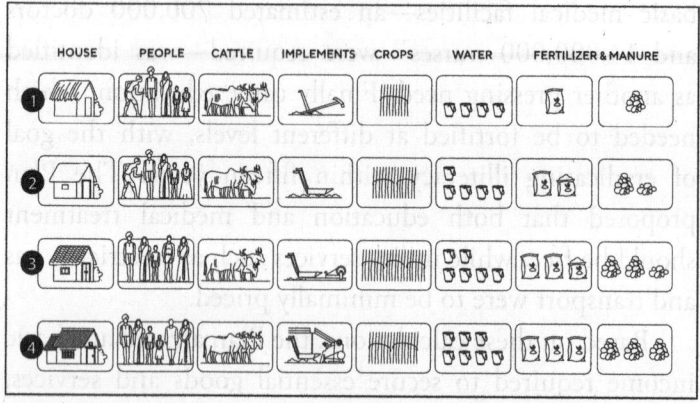

The above illustration depicts what the authors believed could be achieved in agriculture as a result of their Plan. Thatched huts would be replaced by beautiful brick cottages, cattle would be well fed, the wooden plough would be replaced by an iron one and the peasant would also possess a charkha and an electric machine. Water, fertilizer and manure would be plentiful for everyone in the village. Agricultural output would see a 130 per cent rise.

The 'three leaps'

A phased approach in three five-year periods, or three 'leaps', was proposed for achieving the Plan's ambitious goals.[26] In the first leap, the distribution of capital to basic industry and the consumer goods industry would receive maximum importance, while smaller amounts would be allocated to communications and services. A substantial portion was to be earmarked towards importing technology to reduce the 'limited volume of external finance' available.[27] The first five years were expected to be the most challenging, since 'we have been at a standstill for so long'. In the second five-year 'leap', it was envisaged that basic industry would receive an even larger appropriation. In the third 'leap', social services were to be allocated the largest amount, thus allowing them to take a 'terrific leap', while special attention would also be paid to communications.

The 'Three Leaps'

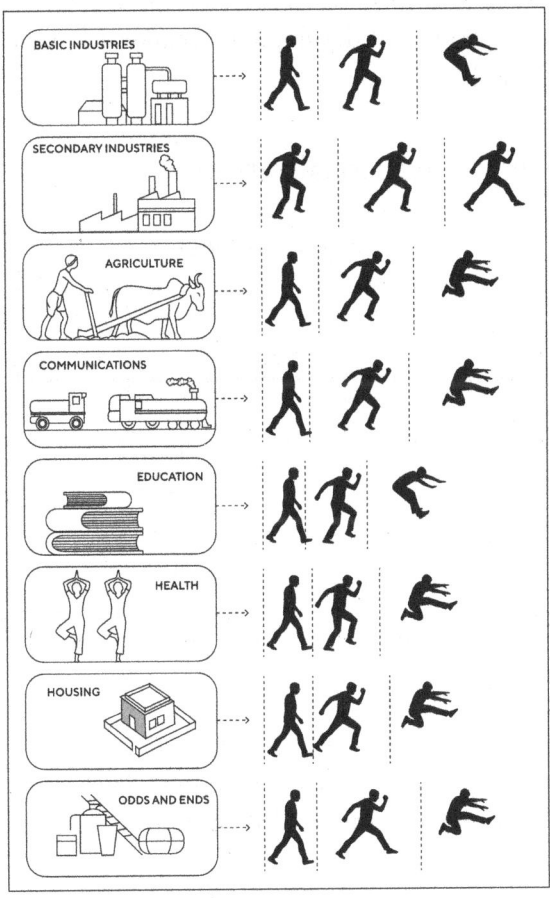

As the basic goods sector developed, it was reasoned, Indian industry would supply the capital goods equipment and machinery which enterprises needed and, in this way, lessen dependence on external finance. Simultaneously, it was hoped, agricultural reform would proceed, though at a slower pace. Industrial development was considered India's primary economic need, and this would also help solve the agrarian problem by increasing the production of consumer goods and developing a market for agricultural raw materials.

A push for industrialization

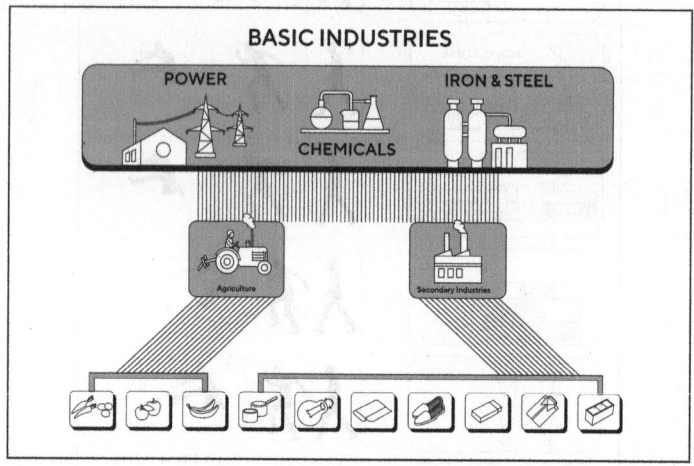

BASIC INDUSTRIES

POWER   IRON & STEEL

CHEMICALS

Agriculture

Secondary Industries

In the authors' vision, the pathway to prosperity lay in rapid industrialization. This was absolutely necessary, since the War years had convinced them that it was the lack of basic machinery and dependence on capital imports that had impeded production and not allowed industry to take optimal advantage of the opportunities that existed.[28] Now, what was needed was a big push towards industrialization, envisaged as the centrepiece of development.

A phased approach was advocated. In the first phase, the focus was to be on key or 'basic industries', as it was on this foundation that India's economic superstructure would rest. The principal constraint of growth, claimed the planners, was shortage of capital compared to the number of people who needed to be employed. They, therefore, championed basic industries, as in the absence of these even simple manufacturing would be held back. 'Not only would such basic industry quicken the pace of industrial development, but would reduce dependence on imports and, as a consequence, on external finance.' Topping their list of basic industries to be promoted was electric power, which would open the 'door to economic development'. Historically, India had lagged far behind in this sector. Although potential power reserves were estimated at about 27 million kilowatts, yet no more than half a million had been developed.[29] Other 'key' basic industries were seen as mining—especially coal, manganese and mica—metallurgy, iron and steel, engineering, chemicals, armaments, transport and cement. So important were these 'key' segments that one-third of the Bombay Plan's total outlay was allocated to basic industry.[30]

Though power and capital goods were prioritized, consumer goods industries such as textiles, glass, leather goods, paper and oil would also be supported. The underlying rationale was to prevent hardship, keep away inflation, provide employment, economize on capital resources and reduce the need for external capital. Cottage industries were deemed to hold a special place. Firstly, they were regarded as providing a better return on money invested since they did not require expensive plants and machinery or large sums of working capital. Secondly, they held 'higher social value' because a large part of the 'consumers' rupees' would go directly to the producer. Finally, they provided employment and would 'counter the tendency of highly mechanized large-scale industry to create unemployment'.[31]

The challenge of agriculture

The Bombay Planners reasoned that all their targets and goals for industry would not be of much use if agriculture were to be neglected. For the Plan 'to have any meaning', they knew that the 'peasant has to be given more purchasing power'.[32] As with industry, agricultural production was also to be boosted, though its target was deliberately 'fixed low', at 130 per cent, or just more than double.[33] An underlying assumption was that agriculture was subject to diminishing returns while industrialization would allow for surplus rural labour to be employed. Although the Plan was biased towards industry, its authors admitted that agriculture would continue to remain the predominant occupation. The initial emphasis was on growing crops

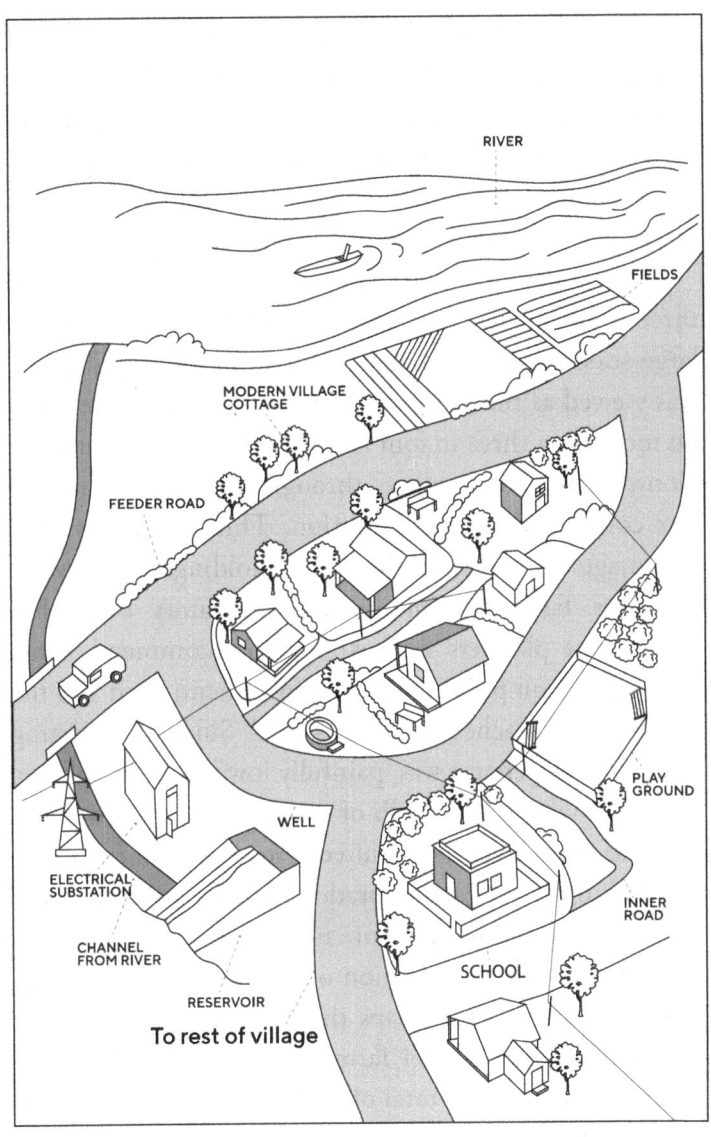

RIVER

FIELDS

MODERN VILLAGE COTTAGE

FEEDER ROAD

PLAY GROUND

WELL

INNER ROAD

ELECTRICAL SUBSTATION

CHANNEL FROM RIVER

RESERVOIR

SCHOOL

To rest of village

necessary for feeding the population. Thus, the overall acreage of cereals, pulses, vegetables, fruits, etc., was to be determined keeping in view the per capita requirements of a nutritive diet. In contrast, the production of commercial crops like tea, jute, cotton, oilseeds, etc. would be adjusted according to trends in international trade.

In the planners' view, agricultural production faced three main challenges: small and fragmented holdings, large-scale rural indebtedness and soil erosion. The first was viewed as the most daunting, as holdings were often no more than three to four acres and frequently scattered. Consolidation of holdings through cooperative farming was considered the best solution. This would have the advantage of increasing the size of holdings to allow for intensive farming while giving cultivators ownership rights. The planners were willing to recommend 'some measure of compulsion' in its enforcement; such was the importance attached to this issue.[34] Since the existing average yield per acre was 'painfully low' at '784 lb of rice, 717 lb of wheat, and 90 lb of cotton',[35] an improvement in yield was urgently required. Accordingly, improved methods of farming, crop rotation and sustained irrigation through the harnessing of new hydroelectric power facilities and the construction of canals were some of the proposed measures. Perhaps the most radical suggestion was to introduce model farms: one farm for every ten villages, making for a total of 65,000 farms. These would be charged with the task of educating the area's villagers and provided with improved varieties of seed, manure and agricultural implements. In all, Rs 845 crore was allocated as non-recurring expenditure for measures to increase agricultural output. Of this, Rs 200 crore was earmarked for soil conservation, Rs 400 crore for canal irrigation works, Rs 50 crore for wells and Rs 195 crore for the development of model farms. In addition, a sum of Rs 400 crore was set aside towards recurring expenditure for these different purposes.[36]

The second issue of debt was considered easier to resolve, thanks to the rise in agricultural prices in the aftermath of the War. The planners estimated that agricultural debt had come down from Rs 1200 crore in 1931[37] and, in one view, 'could not at any rate be more than Rs 200 crore at the most'.[38] However, the planners thought it prudent not to specify any figure, given the lack of precise data.[39] What was apparent was that 'in some parts of the country there is no indebtedness at all', while in other areas 'there may be small debt'. Among the group, Birla was especially optimistic. He had been contending for some time that after the distress caused during the Depression years, the war-related rise in agricultural prices heralded a welcome change in the countryside. At least 30 per cent of the population, he argued, had benefited from rising prices. 'To talk, therefore, of wiping out debt is to talk in the old language.'[40] In the light of such views, rural indebtedness did not worry the planners too much. They felt rural debt could be addressed by cooperative societies once they were provided with long-term finance.[41] So optimistic were they about the efficiency of cooperative societies that the capital outlay of the Plan did not even include the financing required for this.

To deal with the problem of soil erosion, a more long-standing concern, a capital outlay of Rs 200 crore and a recurring sum of Rs 10 crore was allocated. This money was to be used for terracing arable lands, launching afforestation schemes and other suitable measures to prevent large acreages of valuable top soil from being washed away by the rains.[42]

Part II of the Bombay Plan took up the issues of land tenure and land revenue systems. Drawing upon the recommendations of the Bengal Land Revenue Commission (Floud Commission) of 1939, the planners advocated a gradual replacement of the zamindari (often absent feudal landlords leased out their enormous holdings to rentier cultivators) with the ryotwari system (land was owned by the individual cultivator). To achieve this changeover, the state would be required to assume the landlord's functions, pay the landlord rent, and finally offer the landlord payment to settle all claims. Caution was to be exercised to ensure that transfer of land did not occur from cultivators to non-cultivators. Although the planners critiqued the zamindari system and suggested a gradual implementation of the Floud Commission's recommendations, they also acknowledged that the actual cultivator under the zamindari system was often the proprietor of the land for all practical purposes. In reality, however, protection afforded under tenancy laws was available to a very small section of cultivators because of the prevalence of subinfeudation and an hierarchy of middlemen.

Along with the change in land tenure that was intended to create a new class of peasant proprietors, the Plan called for reforming the land revenue system with a uniform basis of assessment across India. This was to ensure a degree of consistency in payment of land revenue, even though flexibility would be required to accommodate fluctuating prices. Fixing an exemption limit for agricultural income and subjecting the surplus to income tax was also suggested.[43] All these measures were expected to result in a substantial increase in national income. Though reform of land tenure was talked about and was undoubtedly the most radical proposal of the Plan, the idea was not developed in depth and the focus still remained, as indicated earlier, on cooperative farming, reduction of rural indebtedness and prevention of soil erosion.

Trends in trade

It was envisaged that once agriculture and industry were on a growth path, a 200 per cent increase in trade and services would follow.[44] The planners placed their hopes on the buoyancy of the internal markets and recommended measures to integrate them by removing all bottlenecks to trade. Most important were the improvements sought in transportation: expanding railway mileage by 50 per cent from 41,000 miles to 62,000 miles; doubling the surface transport network from 300,000 miles to 600,000 miles; metalling of 226,000 miles of roads to make them all-season; and boosting coastal shipping in conjunction with port facilities.

While much optimism existed about the potential of internal trade, the Plan did not have great expectations about growth in foreign trade. In fact, foreign trade was almost ignored, as though it was not in consonance with domestic priorities. With regard to agricultural goods, the expectation was that whatever little exports existed would 'diminish in future'.[45] Since the key aim was self-sufficiency in food production and meeting internal demand, the Plan's advice was not to 'aspire in the initial years of planning to export to foreign markets'.[46]

As in food production, the Plan aspired to self-sufficiency in basic industry. Self-sufficiency was understood largely in terms of not relying on external resources for financing of imports and investment, and was calculated by matching domestic supply and demand in every commodity and service. What the planners did not realize was that achieving self-reliance did not require matching domestic supply and demand but required that in aggregate the demand for external resources matched their supplies.

Financing the plan

Since substantial funds were needed to fulfil projections for different sectors of the economy, resource mobilization was an important aspect of the Plan. Over fifteen years, the total capital requirement for achieving the 'basic standards' in the pivotal sectors of industry, agriculture, communications, higher education and health was estimated at Rs 10,000 crore ($27.6 billion). The planners hoped to tap both external and internal sources of finance.

External sources

It was envisaged that funds to the tune of Rs 2600 crore ($8 billion) would be drawn from external sources. These would be acquired through five means:

(a) Hoarded gold;
 Wealth mainly in the form of hoarded gold was estimated at Rs 1000 crore.[47] At least one-third of this, or Rs 300 crore, was expected to come out in the open, and be used for financing the Plan, if incentives were offered. Such incentives were not specified, though it was stated that these would hinge on the post-war scenario. The 1945 edition of the Bombay Plan expressed the hope that hoarded gold would emerge once there was in place a national government, to which 'people are prepared to entrust their savings because they felt it is theirs'.[48]
(b) Availability of an estimated $1 billion of foreign exchange;
(c) The improved balance of trade that would yield at least Rs 600 crore ($1.8 billion);

(d) Sterling balances that would contribute about Rs 1000 crore ($3 billion);[49]

Sterling assets, 'our past savings abroad', were key to financing the Plan, as they were expected to pay for the sorely needed plant equipment and machinery and technical know-how. Ideally, sterling was to be convertible.[50] 'We should buy these things wherever we can get them, when we want them, and at the cheapest price . . . we shall have to see that our British debtors do not succeed in getting a monopoly.'[51]

(e) An external loan (mainly from the US) of Rs 700 crore ($2 billion) to fill any gaps in financing. Such borrowing would be accompanied with the caveat that the 'creditors do not try to lay down any conditions which might interfere with the complete political and economic freedom of our country'.[52]

Domestic financing

The Plan assumed that maintaining a savings rate of 6 per cent of annual income would yield Rs 4000 crore over a period of fifteen years. However, this was not seen to be sufficient. To address the shortfall, the planners relied on 'created money', or deficit financing. Significantly, the Bombay Plan architects were the only Indian policymakers at that time who placed their trust in Keynesian deficit financing. This, it was reasoned, would expand the quantity of money in circulation, which would add to effective demand, ultimately leading to increased income and employment. The 'created money', in turn, would push up domestic investment and promote rapid industrialization. Public expenditure would also help avoid cyclical depression and economic slumps. Large-scale deficit financing would enable government funding of urgently needed public works, allow resource mobilization and state intervention in crucial investment decisions. The planners expected to raise Rs 3400 crore from the Reserve Bank by borrowing against ad hoc securities. But new money to this extent could be created only if people had 'full confidence in the resources and *bona fides* of the government'.[53] The planners conceded that deficit financing could lead to an inflationary situation and exacerbate existing levels of inequality. Therefore, to keep these in check, in the first fifteen years of intensive planning, 'practically every aspect of economic life will have to be so rigorously controlled by Government that individual liberty and freedom of enterprise will suffer a temporary eclipse'.[54]

The Plan's 'panacea' of deficit financing came to be widely critiqued by economists as dangerous, especially given the post-war inflationary situation. In response, the Planners re-emphasized the role of savings. In a rebuttal note, Birla changed the required savings estimate from the original 6 per cent to an 'annual savings of 16 per cent'. 'I think for a gigantic plan like this, the assumption is not in any way frightening.'[55] It was possible to assume such a jump, he argued, because of the attention given to consumption goods in the initial fifteen years. He further contended that the savings rate could be raised without adversely affecting consumption. Of course, deficit financing would be accompanied with effective price control and rationing. How such savings would be tapped was elaborated by Lokanathan, who forwarded several options such as 'taxation, direct restrictions on consumption, allocation to reserves in state-owned and controlled businesses, special allowances from taxation in reporting allocations to reserves', etc. The real issue for the planners was 'how much control' would be required and 'how much control can or should the public stand'.[56]

'How are things to be shared?'[57]

After setting various fifteen-year sectoral targets and establishing their modes of financing, one important issue the planners discussed in Part II of the Bombay Plan, *Distribution—Role of the State*, was how to share the benefits of the envisaged increase in production. This was especially pertinent in the light of the Plan's declared intention of reducing inequality. Two sets of measures were proposed in the 1945 edition of the Bombay Plan: 'levelling up' was to raise the general income of the lower-income groups, while 'levelling down' implied a reduction in the cost of living and 'over-consumption' by the higher-income classes.

Of the two approaches, 'levelling up' demanded greater attention as it encapsulated measures to boost full employment, increase efficiency, increase wages, secure fair agricultural prices, promote multipurpose cooperatives and implement land reform. Fundamental to many of the ills plaguing India was the problem of unemployment. The Plan was influenced by the ideas of the economist William Henry Beveridge, then director of LSE, who was trying to recalibrate the relationship between market and the state in the UK, and whose ideas were to become the basis of the post-war welfare state. The Bombay Planners' proposals, however, were not as far-reaching as those of Beveridge. In his 1943 publication, *Pillars of Security and Other War-Time Essays*, Beveridge justified the need for social security by issuing a clarion call against the 'five giant evils' of 'want, disease, ignorance, squalor and idleness'. To Beveridge, idleness was an evil as insidious as disease and squalor, and he urged for determined action from the government to create work. Agreeing with Beveridge on the need to destroy 'the giant Idleness', the planners advocated a raft of measures for the industrial and agrarian sectors.[58] In industry, they expectedly favoured less capital-intensive units that would allow the employment of more workers per unit of capital than was usually the case in industrialized countries. They also recommended that small-scale and cottage industries be encouraged to maximize employment opportunities, especially in the context of rural unemployment. Largely a seasonal phenomenon, rural unemployment could be mitigated by the establishment of industries such as spinning and weaving, paper-making, shoe-making, basket-weaving, soap-making and tanning. Mixed farming and multicropping were other measures suggested to alleviate seasonal rural unemployment.

The authors of the Bombay Plan also drew upon Keynes, who contended that the availability of jobs and the supply of unemployed workers would not be balanced in the short run by economic forces but would need state intervention. Favouring a Keynesian fiscal stimulus, they backed state spending on public works, especially to tackle seasonal agricultural unemployment. In their view, such a stimulus would provide a 'very substantial increase' in employment.[59]

Another significant 'levelling up' measure was the proposal for a minimum wage. This would be easier to implement for factory workers, as the fixing of the minimum wage could be entrusted to separate committees for each industry. For agricultural labour, a minimum wage for 'each region in the country'[60] was proposed. Together, such measures were expected to increase the average income of agricultural workers by 50 per cent, of industrial workers by 93 per cent and of workers in the services sector by 129 per cent.[61]

The planners believed that a rise in monetary income would be enough to ensure a minimum standard of living for the poorest sections of the population. To achieve this minimum standard, they made two additional proposals. First, that educational and medical services be free, and second, that public utility services, including electricity, gas and transport, and communication tools such as radio, telephone, posts and telegraphs be subsidized. Although comprehensive social insurance was considered impractical, health insurance and paid holidays in the organized sectors were recommended, and the possibility of some sort of 'social insurance' in large-scale industry hinted at. The cost of such subsidized benefits, however, was not worked out. For the bulk of the population, help was to be sought during contingencies and natural calamities from a sort of national relief fund.[62]

These 'levelling up' measures were to be accompanied with a 'levelling down' of upper-income groups, the principal means of preventing wide disparities in income. Its main instrument was to be taxation. 'The most important method of preventing gross inequalities is direct taxation, which in effect transfers income from the comparatively richer classes of society to the poorer. A steeply graduated income-tax, which would keep personal incomes within limits, would obviously be the most important weapon for this purpose in the fiscal armoury of the country.'[63] Besides increasing direct taxation, death duties were advised for 'correcting the existing inequalities'. Somewhat hesitatingly (and without dwelling upon this at length), the planners also drew attention towards the 'title-deeds of absentee and parasitic landowners'.

'Who is to do it all?'

'Who is to do it all? Who is to organize the increased production and who is to see to it that the benefits are equitably shared?'[64] In answering these questions, the planners were unequivocal that their vision could only be fulfilled through the energetic intervention of the state. Recognizing the limitations of the market, they proposed an 'enlargement of the positive as well as preventive functions of the state'.

However, they were careful to point out that the interventionist state they had in mind had to be democratic, unlike the two best-known contemporary examples of planned economies, Russia and Germany. There could be no compromise with the 'belief that the freedom of the individual to give full expression to his personality is one of the supreme values of life and among its basic needs'.[65] If a planned economy involved a temporary 'restriction of individual freedom', it would be of 'limited duration and confined to specific purposes'.[66]

The planners contended that the gulf between socialism and capitalism was narrowing; neither existed in a 'pure form', and all economic forms would be a combination of both.[67] They envisaged a 'mixed' economy in which the state and the private sector would have complementary, even interchangeable, roles. Some industrial assets would be owned and managed by the state and others left to private enterprise. Thus, the economy would be 'based on both planning and free enterprise', with the state playing a dominant role till a certain minimum level of human development had been achieved.[68] For such a mixed economy to work, three main principles were to be followed:

a) 'Sufficient scope for the play of individual initiative and enterprise' had to be given;

b) The 'interest of the community should be safeguarded' against the 'abuse of individual freedom';

c) The 'state should play a positive role in directing economic policy and developing economic resources'.[69]

Keeping these principles in mind, the operational framework of the Bombay Plan was capitalism, but a tempered capitalism that gave the state greater influence in the market. As Keynesian enthusiasts, the planners held the view that markets could not be fully trusted, that the economy had no natural propensity to provide full employment, and the state needed to intervene forcefully to boost consumption. Consequently, state intervention in demand management, resource mobilization and public expenditure to generate employment were endorsed. Indeed, the planners believed that state intervention in the manner Keynes had proposed was necessary to safeguard capitalism itself, since its very survival was predicated on a broad base of prosperity which, in turn, was dependent on alleviating inequalities.

The economic functions of the state outlined above, the planners recommended, should be entrusted to technocrats, who would form a new 'economic civil service'. Responsible for implementation of the Plan, this group of personnel would be specially trained to work under a centralized body that would have 'sufficient powers of coordination'.

'Interim period' of intensive, planned development

Making a distinction between the first fifteen years, or 'interim period', 'when the plan was in the process of being carried out', and 'normal times', which were defined as the period by when the 'planned economy had come into normal operation', the planners visualized a significantly larger role for the state in the initial phase, both in terms of ownership and control. The only exception would be small and cottage industries, whose ownership would vest with individuals and cooperatives, and the state's role limited to that of making available to them power, credit, tools and raw materials, and helping them market their produce.[70]

Cottage and small industries apart, in the 'interim period' the planners were willing to go so far as to allow that 'practically every aspect of economic life [would] be so vigorously controlled by government that individual liberty and freedom of enterprise [would] suffer a temporary eclipse'. They argued that the state would need to 'adopt a number of controls of a temporary character', similar to those 'present under war conditions', as without them 'planned economic development' would 'be hardly possible'.[71] So, state intervention was expected in 'production, distribution, consumption, investment, foreign trade and exchange, wages and working conditions'. Such intervention would help ensure regional distribution of industry through the issue of licences for establishing new industries and extending the capacity of existing ones, while the objective of state control over distribution was to determine the usage of raw materials, semi-finished products and capital goods.[72] Controls over consumption would include the setting up of fair-price shops for essential goods and for goods made with state financing, while investment controls essentially meant that new capital issues would need approval by the state. Trade and exchange controls implied 'conserving foreign exchange' and promoting Indian industries, and wage controls would ensure fair conditions for labour and 'efficiency of management'.

Even more than state ownership, it was state control that was emphasized by the planners. The objective was 'mobilization of all the available means of production and their direction towards socially desirable ends'. There remained, however, a lingering fear of excessive state control which found expression in the later edition of the Bombay Plan in 1945.

When the Bombay group was working on the Plan's draft, Friedrich von Hayek's *The Road to Serfdom,* in which he opposes all planning on the ground that it subverts freedom and poses a grave threat to democratic liberties, had not yet been published. In the 1945 edition of the Bombay Plan, however, its authors, clearly influenced by Hayek's libertarian classic that came out in 1944, sounded a warning by invoking his ideas. Almost repudiating their earlier views, they noted:

It has been argued by a learned professor that the path of total planning is the road to serfdom. Is this assumption true that a planned economy can only function within the political framework of dictatorship? Such a fear is natural since in the two countries which have witnessed the most impressive experiments in economic planning undertaken in recent years, namely Soviet Union and Germany, the state has exerted over the activities of its citizens in every sphere of life a degree of authority which provides little scope for the exercise of individual freedom.'[73]

'Normal times'

In 'normal times', the planners argued for a shrinking role for the state which, henceforth, was to be limited to 'coordination of general economic activity'; 'management of currency and public finance'; collection of statistical data and other information; and legislative initiatives to 'safeguard the economically weak classes'.[74]

It was proposed that at all times sectors would be divided into those under state ownership and control and those in which private enterprise would dominate. Ownership and management would be dependent on the nature of the specific enterprise.[75] Thus, state ownership was recommended for sectors important for 'public welfare or security'.[76] Industries related to defence, communications, posts and telegraphs were to be state-owned and controlled as a 'more or less permanent feature'.[77] Further, public utilities and basic industries using scarce natural resources were to be under state control. These checks could take different forms such as price fixation, limitation of dividends, licensing, prescription of work conditions, fixing of wages, nomination of directors on management boards, 'efficiency auditing', etc.

Significantly, the planners proposed that industries owned by the state need not necessarily be managed by the state. They could be run by private enterprises or by ad hoc public corporations, similar to the London Passenger Transport Board. The possibility of both state and private enterprises being involved within the same sector, the intention being to secure 'maximum contribution to the well-being of the community by the industry as a whole', was not ruled out. Taking their cue from the Fabian intellectual G.D.H. Cole, who argued that there was 'no need to socialize at once all the forms of production' and that the lines between socialized production and private enterprise need not be strictly drawn,[78] the Bombay group too recommended that 'within a single branch of production there may be some parts which it is desirable to socialize, and others which are best left under private ownership and control'. The point was less rigidity and leaving room for 'diverse experiments'.[79]

The Bombay Plan may be seen as representing a search for a new type of capitalism. In this search, the authors enlisted the support of various contemporary economists. Though most impressed by Keynes, from whom they drew several of their ideas, we have seen how they also acknowledged the wisdom of other doctrinal paths. The Bombay Plan architects envisaged the compatibility of planning with capitalism, a middle path between central planning and the market, and between state-owned enterprises and private enterprise. They did not see planning as antithetical to or incompatible with a market economy, and their ideas anticipated the East Asian developmental model that became so successful in the 1960s and 1970s.

6

THE PLAN AND THE PUBLIC

Selling the plan

The widespread debate and discussion that the Bombay Plan evoked both in India and overseas went far beyond the expectations of its authors. The Plan, confessed Lokanathan, 'exerted an influence perhaps out of proportion to its undoubted merits'.[1]

This may have had something to do with the publicity blitz that was launched to announce the Plan's publication. Press conferences were held, where the authors boldly fielded questions, advertisements were placed in major newspapers like the *Statesman*,[2] and complimentary review copies dispatched liberally to important individuals (including the viceroy, members of his executive council, secretaries to the government, governors of provinces, premiers of Indian states, members of the central legislature, consuls and trade commissioners, vice chancellors of universities, leading economists) and organizations (the Indian Chamber of Commerce, the Bengal National Chamber of Commerce and FICCI, for instance, were given fifty copies each for distribution). Even leading libraries in the major cities received free copies. And, of course, not to be left out were the Indian nationalist leaders. Devdas Gandhi, then editor of the *Hindustan Times*, ensured that Gandhi and Nehru received their copies.[3]

Every possible opportunity to promote the Plan was seized. At one of the numerous press conferences held at Bombay House, Thakurdas, JRD, Matthai and Shroff explained the Plan's objectives and urged that the authors be seen as 'citizens of the land, irrespective of any consideration about their economic class'.[4] The authors met with government officials, made efforts to enlist the support of Indian political leaders and spoke at public events. In a bid to reach out to as wide an audience as possible, Shroff spoke to the Bombay Indian Progressive Group; Thakurdas addressed the Rotary Club; and Matthai held a discussion with the Bombay Women's Council.[5] A joint meeting was organized for members of important commercial bodies, including the Indian Chamber of Commerce, the Bengal National Chamber of Commerce, the Marwari Chamber of Commerce and the Muslim Chamber, where Dalal explained the Plan and responded to criticism.[6]

The printing, distribution and marketing of the Bombay Plan had been entrusted to the newly established public relations department of Tata Sons. Set up in

1943, the PR outfit was the brainchild of Minoo Masani, former general secretary of the Congress Socialist Party who had recently joined the Tatas in 1941 as secretary of Tata Chemicals and, from 1943 onwards, headed the PR department.[7] The first edition was printed by an in-house Tata enterprise, the Commercial Printing Press, at Cowasji Patel Street, Fort, Bombay. Masani took great care to ensure that there was no leakage of the contents to ensure a 'friendly reception to the Plan in the press generally'. The Plan was translated into several Indian languages to ensure as wide a readership as possible. While the rights to the Hindi edition were given to another publisher, the Urdu, Gujarati, Tamil, Kannada and Bengali translations were handled in-house. The total expenditure added up to Rs 15,000 and, although it had been earlier decided that the businessmen-authors in the group would share the costs, an excited JRD insisted on paying one-third of the total.

Enthused by the initial sales of the Plan, JRD persuaded his fellow authors that an 'illustrated popular' edition should be published. The task was assigned to Masani, whose recently published *Our India*, with striking illustrations by C.H.G. Moorhouse, had sold over 500,000 copies by then.[8] The Bombay Plan's popular edition was to be along similar lines, with many attractive visuals and charts.[9] Birla alerted JRD about the need to carefully choose pictures and charts with 'an Indian background' in order to 'appeal to the Indian public'.[10] It was decided that this edition would not be published in-house, and

Oxford University Press, which had brought out Masani's *Our India*, was approached.[11] This illustrated edition, with over thirty-eight coloured drawings by Moorhouse, titled *Picture of a Plan*, was published in late 1945.[12] *Picture of a Plan* explored the underlying ideas of the Bombay Plan in five chapters. The first looked at 'Our Needs'; the second, titled 'After Fifteen Years', discussed what the Plan would lead to; the third addressed the question of resources: 'Where are the men and money to come from?'; the fourth, 'How are things to be shared?', looked at distribution; and the final chapter, 'Who is to do it all?', examined the role of the state.

So extensive was the publicity work related to the Plan that, right up to 1946, the PR department of the Tatas was mainly engaged in plan-related activity.[13] An enthusiastic JRD kept a close eye on all the department's work, making suggestions about publicity measures and personally responding to queries about distribution of the Plan's copies.

Reception of the Plan

'A best-seller',[14] the Plan's initial copies flew off the shelves. In Calcutta alone, no less than 350 copies were ordered initially by individuals.[15] A second print run was hurriedly done in January 1944 itself, followed by reprints in February, March, June and August. Talks were started with Penguin for the publication of a UK edition: in June 1944, Part I of the Bombay Plan was published as a

Penguin Special, and later the two parts of the Plan were compiled together into one book by Penguin UK.

Thanks to all these editions—and the publicity surrounding them—the Plan attracted widespread attention. Long and detailed reviews by the Bombay-based economists P.A. Wadia and K.T. Merchant appeared in the *Bombay Chronicle* and *Hindustan Weekly*, and national newspapers like the *Statesman* and the *Times of India* too exhaustively analysed the Plan.

The international press too took heed of the Plan. The *New York Times* commended the Plan's authors for their 'enlightened self-interest' to propose India's regeneration by tackling the fundamental problems of poverty.[16] The *Washington Post* declared the Plan's aim as no less than 'revolutionizing India',[17] while the *Chicago Daily Tribune*[18] noted, pointedly, the Plan's dependence on American imports to aid industrialization. In Britain, press reviews of the Plan were similarly enthusiastic. Describing it as 'the most widely read social document of recent years in India', the *Times* declared that 'Indian public interest in post-war planning has already been brought to a high-pitch'[19] by its publication. The *Observer*,[20] *Manchester Guardian*,[21] *Yorkshire Post*,[22] and *Glasgow Herald*[23] were among the papers that analysed the plan threadbare. *The Economist* said the Plan's 'easy assumption that there will be an Indian government, responsible, national and efficient, is the biggest "if" of all'.[24]

The Plan created quite a stir in official colonial circles. In London, it came up for debate in the House of Commons.

Labour member Lord Sorenson asked Amery, the secretary of state for India, if the Government of India was likely to incorporate the Bombay Plan's proposals in its own scheme for post-war reconstruction.[25] Schuster, former finance member and a close friend of Birla's, 'welcomed' the Plan and urged the government to use the opportunity this afforded to discuss its own plans for reconstruction with Indians.

In India, the tone was set by the viceroy, Lord Wavell. He publicly proclaimed that, while there may be differences between the Bombay Plan and the administration about ideas of economic development, the aims of the Planners were, in principle, identical with his own, namely, that they both shared the objective of ensuring a substantial increase in the standard of living in India. He further indicated that he was considering measures for strengthening the government's own planning organization.[26] The viceroy charged his economic advisor, Sir Theodore Gregory, with the task of articulating an official response to the Plan.[27] In his budget speech in March 1944, the finance member, Sir Jeremy Raisman, commended the Plan as a useful document while critiquing its financial assumptions; and a month later, he and other senior officials, including the supply member, Ramaswami Mudaliar, met the Planners.

The serious consideration that the colonial state gave to the Plan became even more manifest when the Planners were invited to meet members of the reconstruction committee of the viceroy's executive council, headed by Sir J.P Srivastava. In a four-hour meeting at Srivastava's home, the planners explained their ideas.[28] That evening, the viceroy offered Dalal, one of the eight signatories to the Bombay Plan, charge of the planning portfolio in his executive council.[29] In June 1944, Wavell decided to establish a new department of planning and development, and Dalal was formally appointed as the department's head and member of the viceroy's executive council.[30] Dalal's appointment clearly signalled that the Bombay Plan ideas and colonial views about post-war reconstruction could be reconciled, and 'a scheme embodying the best of both sets of ideas can be evolved and worked'.[31] The other authors of the Plan, however, were not enthused by Dalal's appointment. JRD, on being asked by Wavell to release Dalal from Tata Sons, actually said the firm could not spare him.[32] An annoyed Birla thought Dalal 'had no business to accept the job' and 'never showed the courtesy of consulting us when he was offered the job'.[33] Meanwhile, provincial governments were asked to set up their own planning departments that would work closely with the new central department in Delhi.

It wasn't bouquets all the way for the Bombay Plan. Many brickbats were thrown at it too. When it came up for discussion in November 1944 in the central legislative assembly, the Aligarh-based economist and member of the Muslim League, Sir Zia-ud-Din Ahmed, argued that the Plan should not be considered in the House since it was 'the outcome of an unholy alliance between Indian and foreign capitalists'. He contended that adoption of the Plan's proposals would 'ultimately destroy the cottage industries' and was the 'shortest route to turn India into a Bolshevik country'.[34] His chief objection was to the Plan's premise of a federal scheme of governance with a strong centre. From the Congress benches, N.G. Ranga alleged that cottage industries and rural interests had been neglected in the Plan, a point strongly refuted by Dalal. T.T.A. Chetty moved an amendment, on behalf of the Congress, that a non-official committee be appointed to examine the Bombay Plan along with other proposed blueprints, including the Visvesvaraya Plan[35] and M.N. Roy's 'People's Plan'. When asked by assembly members if the government had accepted the Bombay Plan, Dalal replied that while the objective had been accepted, in so far as it related to raising the standard of living and increasing purchasing power, the government was devising its own scheme.[36] True to his word, the following year, on 21 April 1945, the government issued its *Statement of Government's Industrial Policy*, which reflected the influence of the Bombay Plan. The economist Vera Anstey noted pointedly that 'there is little doubt that the recent quickening of the tempo of such planning can be partially attributed to the Bombay Plan'.[37]

Through all the debate and discussion on the Plan in various quarters, what exercised the planners the most was Mahatma Gandhi's reaction to it. Anxious to get his endorsement, they were very nervous about the Mahatma's response since his disdain for planning was well known. They felt a careful strategy had to be worked out to present the Plan to him. A copy was dispatched to him while he was imprisoned at the Aga Khan Palace in Poona.[38] After Gandhi's release, Thakurdas, JRD and Birla paid him a 'courtesy call' to inquire about his health, at Juhu, Bombay, in early June 1944. Only a passing reference was made to the Plan as the Mahatma was still recuperating after his fast.[39]

In the weeks that followed, there were worrisome newspaper reports that Shriman Narayan Agarwal, son-in-law of the industrialist Jamnalal Bajaj and a professed Gandhian who was then teaching at Wardha College, visited Gandhi in the hill station of Panchgani in early August 1944 and extensively discussed the Plan with him. Meanwhile, A.N. Agarwala, who taught at Allahabad University, separately wrote *A Critique of the Industrialists' Plan*[40] in which he asserted that the Bombay Plan was limited in scope since it focused excessively on industrial development and overlooked sectors such as agriculture, trade, banking, insurance and transport. He also claimed that the Planners were too complacent in their belief that the sterling balances accumulating with the Reserve Bank of India would be made available to finance development. More disturbingly, there was information that Agarwal himself was in the process of writing a plan. There were also rumours that K.T. Shah, secretary of the Congress's national planning committee, formed in 1938, whose 'hostility to the Plan' was well known, had discussed it with Gandhi. No one could predict how the Mahatma would respond.

It worried JRD that there was 'always a chance that, under the spur of such discussions, he may give expression to some views of which maximum capital would be made by any interested parties anxious to discredit us'. One option was to meet him during his forthcoming visit to Bombay, when he was scheduled to hold talks with the Muslim League leader Mohammed Jinnah. But it was felt that such a meeting would attract undue publicity since Gandhi would be surrounded by the media.[41] Thakurdas, JRD and Matthai, who were all based in Bombay, agreed that the best man for sounding out Gandhi's opinion was Birla. As JRD told Birla: 'Of all of us, you are much the closest to Gandhiji, and you will best know the right way of handling the matter.'[42] Birla had already met Gandhi, who had told him 'that he liked it' (the Plan) though they had not had a detailed discussion. Birla assured his colleagues that he would fix a meeting with the Mahatma.[43]

The Planners' fears were not unfounded, as they soon discovered that Gandhi had written a foreword for Agarwal's book, *The Gandhian Plan of Economic Development for India*. Like other Gandhian economists, Agarwal was no admirer of the Bombay Plan, which he condemned as 'essentially a capitalist plan on western lines'.[44] Disturbingly, in his foreword, Gandhi commended Agarwal's plan as one 'in full sympathy with the way of life for which I stand'.[45]

Critique by economists and the Planners' response

Criticism emerged from other quarters too. Shah, an economist known to be close to the Congress leadership, was amongst the first to make a scathing critique of the Plan. Left-leaning economists too weighed in vehemently. B.N. Banerjea of Calcutta University condemned it as an *Alphabet of Fascist Economics*.[46] Roy did not mince words either, calling the Plan 'the programme of Indian Fascism'.[47] Roy criticized the Bombay Plan on several issues, including its emphasis on industry, its financial proposals that were deemed inflationary, and its use of savings to finance development. He also argued that although raising the standard of living was one of the Plan's objectives, it failed to recommend ways to do so explicitly. In his view, the main objective of the Bombay Plan seemed to be to increase production, and not to ensure the well-being of the people. He also believed that the Plan perpetuated the status quo of the capitalist economy, benefiting only big business, and did not concern itself with the equitable distribution of wealth.[48] G.D. Parikh's main bone of contention in 'The Master Plan X-Rayed'[49] was that the Bombay Plan 'does not visualize any change in the existing status quo'. Much like the others, Parikh faulted the Plan's bias towards industry and its emphasis on sterling balances and 'created money' as modes of financing. He also argued that foreign borrowing could lead to foreign interference in the country. The state would then have to assume a totalitarian character in order to establish the internal stability needed to assure foreign investors of the security of their investments. This, he feared, could eventually lead to the foundation of fascism. Wadia and Merchant, both professors of economics at Bombay University, alleged that the Plan betrayed a 'bourgeoisie mentality' and was a 'crude, halting, half-hearted compromise between capitalism and a collectivist organization of society'.[50] Like Roy, they too believed that the Bombay Plan did not concern itself with equitable distribution of wealth, thus leaving the masses open to exploitation, and that individual gain remained the driving force of the Plan. Another drawback, they argued, was the Plan's bias towards industrial production and its dismissive attitude towards agriculture.

Such widespread criticism worried the Planners. In August 1944, Birla wrote to JRD:

> . . . I wonder if you agree with me that the real hostility is not against the Plan so much, but against the businessman in general. The main target of attack is the businessman and the critics treat yourself and myself as a symbol of the business community. The Communists, the Socialists, the British vested interests and our own government all seem to be on common ground. Sir Ramaswami Mudaliar's recent speech in south India frightening people of "big combines" was in the same tune. There is, as if it were, a plan to discredit businessmen. Their patriotism, integrity and good motives are questioned. People are told that schemes for more Tatanagars and Birlanagars are afoot. First iconoclasm and then the next step, that is the technique of these critics. We should, therefore, tackle the root cause and not merely beat about the branches and bushes.[51]

The more serious criticism of the Plan related to its financial provisions. The Plan was faulted on several counts: its projections were based on pre-war price levels; it overlooked annual costs (which would add to capital costs); it viewed gold as external finance; it looked at the balance of trade in isolation and not as part of the income and savings of the nation; and its proposed use of the Reserve Bank's sterling assets would undermine the currency standard of India, among other things. There was scepticism regarding the suggestion that two-thirds of the Plan could be financed by savings, foreign assets and foreign loans, leaving one-third to be met by 'created money'. The planners were also accused of underestimating the inflationary risks arising from their own estimates.[52] B.R. Shenoy suspected miscalculation to the extent of 'double counting, or even counting three times over' of savings, considering that the planners viewed savings, balance of trade and 'created money' as independent sources of obtaining capital for investment.[53]

Most of the criticism centred on the concept of 'created money' and its inflationary risk. The critique led Birla to admit that the Planners had gone 'wrong in treating the subject from a traditional point of view in terms of created money, rather than in terms of planned savings'. He reworked the argument to say that that 'whether you call it savings, or balance of trade, or created money, what is required is savings to the extent of 16 per cent of the national income in the period'.[54]

The planners were also censured for first setting unrealistic targets and then examining how they could be achieved. Many experts claimed that agricultural output could not be increased by more than 30 per cent, as opposed to the 130 per cent envisaged by the planners. Similarly, the Plan estimate of 6 per cent domestic savings seemed too high. In the critics' view, it was also 'unreasonable to count upon full repayment' of sterling debts within fifteen years.[55]

Industrialists' delegation to the UK and the USA, 1945

Even as the Plan was being drawn up, Birla had kept top officialdom apprised of all the deliberations under way. Soon after Lord Wavell arrived in India as viceroy in 1943, Birla took an early opportunity to give him an update. Later, when he met Sir E.M. Jenkins, private secretary to Wavell, he proposed that a delegation of Indian industrialists be sent to England to discuss post-war reconstruction and explore areas of technical collaboration with their counterparts in Britain.[56] Much to his delight, Wavell announced a plan for such a delegation soon afterwards.

The publication of the Bombay Plan a few months later further advanced this idea of an Indian industrial mission and generated substantial interest both at home and overseas. Several businesspersons expressed a desire to be part of this mission to England and America 'for general inspection of factories with a view to making purchases of capital goods eventually'.[57] Many also saw this as an opportunity to place orders for capital equipment and war-surplus stock.[58] From amongst the planners, it was initially decided that JRD, Birla and Kasturbhai would be part of the delegation. Eventually, Kasturbhai opted out and Shroff joined in. While a list of other potential invitees was being worked out, a number of influential persons showed interest in joining the mission. Nehru's sister Krishna Hutheesing, for instance, wanted her husband to accompany the mission as secretary. She asked JRD, a close friend, to intercede, but her request was politely turned down on the ground that the decision lay with the government.[59] Eventually, Lokanathan accompanied the seven-member delegation as secretary. Besides JRD, Birla and Shroff, the number of delegates who were to be part of the mission was whittled down to four businessmen and their nine technical advisers.[60]

A week before the proposed departure of the industrial mission, however, controversy overtook it from an unexpected quarter. Gandhi, then at Mahabaleshwar, told the *Bombay Chronicle* how poorly he thought of the delegation. He alleged that 'big merchants, capitalists, industrialists and others speak and write against the Government but in action do its will and even profit through it—though the profit may amount to, say, five per cent against the Government's 95.' He sternly warned that the 'so-called unofficial deputation . . . dare not proceed, whether for inspection or for entering into a shameful deal as long as the moving spirits of the Working Committee are being detained without trial for the sole crime of sincerely striving for India's independence.'[61] Shocked at the Mahatma's bombshell, the delegates responded hastily. Birla telegraphed him that he was 'much pained' by his 'public expression of mistrust in the bona-fides of myself, Tata and Kasturbhai whom you have known so well'.[62] JRD defended himself through a press statement, saying that the Mahatma had committed a 'grave injustice'. It was 'a thousand pities' that he had not even 'obtained a clarification of our aims before giving public expression to his views'.[63] The storm, fortunately, subsided in a few days, with Gandhi writing individually to some of the members to pacify them.[64] He clarified that if they were not going to enter into deals or 'commit' themselves, then he granted them his 'blessings and prayers in terms of famishing and naked India.'[65] On being queried about his 'conditional blessings', Gandhi defended them as 'being the only way that ahimsa can act'. He had given his consent but placed them all (the Planners) 'on their honour' and believed his 'blessings will haunt like a ghost anyone who contravenes conditions attached to it'.[66] He entrusted Birla with the task of pacifying Tata and his other angry colleagues.[67]

The mission, at last, proceeded as planned.[68] Leaving Karachi in the third week of May 1945, it spent five weeks in Britain, then six weeks in the USA, returning to London in the second week of August before arriving home at the end of the month.

The delegates were received warmly in both countries by officials and industrialists. In England, they met government officials, including Lord Amery, secretary of state for India since 1940, Lord Halifax, former viceroy of India, Lord Pethick-Lawrence, prominent Labour politician who succeeded Amery as secretary of state for India in 1945, and Sir George Schuster, former finance member of the viceroy's council. Schuster had been especially helpful in enlisting support for the mission and was instrumental in bringing together a group of fifty industrialists in the Midlands in preparation for the visit.[69] Individually, the delegates found themselves flooded with invitations to visit factories. Birla alone had received over 200 letters of invitation 'from every nook and corner' in England.[70] With the help of H.M. Patel and T.C. Boyd, civil servants in the department of industries and civil supplies, as well as Dalal, contact had been established with British manufacturers, and lists of machinery that would be required in different Indian sectors after the War had been prepared.[71] Several meetings were held with members of the Federation of British Industries, the London Chamber of Commerce and the Association of British Chambers of Commerce.

In the USA, the mission's reception was equally cordial. The delegates met influential officials in Washington such as Henry Wallace (secretary of state for commerce), William Thorpe (deputy to the assistant secretary of state, in charge of economic affairs), Amos Taylor (director, bureau of foreign and domestic commerce), Frank Waring (assistant to the secretary of commerce) and Wayne Chatfield Taylor (president, Export-Import Bank of Washington). The delegation asked Taylor if the US might be prepared to give a loan to India for two years till the issue of dollar exchange was solved.[72] The 'crowning function' was a luncheon reception hosted by Dean Acheson, who was then with the division of cultural cooperation in the State Department.[73] In New York, meetings were held with many banks, including National City Bank, Chase National Bank and the House of Morgan. In many of the meetings, the lead was taken by Birla, Sarkar and Shroff. At these gatherings, Shroff argued that the Plan presented 'a splendid opportunity for the United States to enter the Indian market'. 'The only fly in the ointment is our difficulty of getting American dollars to pay.'[74] Such was the demand for the Plan's copies in the USA that Shroff told the press he was going to reprint 10,000 copies for distribution.[75] An important issue raised was of the sterling balances, and that India's 'urgent post-War needs both of rehabilitation and expansion could not be met, unless a portion of the blocked balances was made convertible into dollars and other hard currencies.'

The delegates lobbied hard both in the UK and the USA, and found—not surprisingly—that the Americans were more sympathetic to their pleas that India should be released from the empire sterling pool.[76] They urged influential State Department officials and members of the House of Representatives to support this demand, arguing that America could also help by extending credit loans to the British to make available part of India's blocked sterling in dollars.[77] Other notable meetings were with the celebrated author Pearl S. Buck and with David Lilienthal, chairman of the Tennessee Valley Authority. The latter showcased to the Indians a completely different perspective of planning, in which the emphasis was on a 'region' (Tennessee Valley) as the ideal unit and not on the state's central authority.

Apart from the scheduled group conclaves, the delegates spent much of their time meeting separately with individuals and organizations to discuss areas of collaboration in line with their own business interests. In these meetings, they discovered that whole factories in the mid-West, with unused surplus machinery, could be bought immediately.[78] All sorts of things were on sale, 'from pins and gloves to big plants', Birla wrote to his brother Braj Mohan.[79] In sectors such as textiles, machinery was ready for assembly and would cost no more than $1,000,000 to $2,000,000 for an entire factory.[80] Of course, the big hurdle was obtaining foreign exchange in dollars. Whenever the opportunity arose, the delegates pressed home the point that India's sterling credits could be used.[81] But, since the War was still to end officially, the industrialists found that it was primarily a sellers' market and they would have to wait a while for final deals.[82]

Widely circulated in India and overseas, the Bombay Plan generated a lively public debate and caused a stir in intellectual, political and economic circles in India. It impacted government thinking, as can be seen in the decision to set up a department of planning. The colonial government not only began to consider the question of post-war reconstruction seriously, it co-opted Dalal, one of the eight authors of the Plan, as head of the newly established planning department.

7

AFTERLIFE OF THE PLAN

Six years after the publication of the Bombay Plan, independent India embarked upon its 'adventure' of planning, and there were great expectations from the Planning Commission, the institution founded with great fanfare in January 1950. The commission's brief was to assess the country's resources, prioritize investment proposals and formulate plans for the most effective use of resources for national economic reconstruction. Prime Minister Nehru announced that it had the 'highest importance and status' and was to be 'a top-ranking body with a great deal of authority and prestige'.[1] Its members were given the rank of ministers of state and its deputy chairman that of a Cabinet minister. Nehru became the commission's chairman, which led to an immediate increase in its standing as the pre-eminent economic policy-making body of the nation. A year after its founding, the commission published the First Plan draft outline in July 1951, followed by a final version in December 1952.

First Five-Year Plan

Notwithstanding all the hype that accompanied the formation of the Planning Commission, its First Five-Year Plan was a modest document. In contrast to the Bombay Plan, there was no talk of doubling the per capita income within fifteen years. Nor did it lay down growth targets in terms of national income or standards of living.[2] The Bombay Plan had been far more ambitious with its ideas of equitable growth, its focus on the centrality of the state and its push to promote capital industry. No such promises were forthcoming in the First Plan. Its main concern was no more than 'effectuating the post-War and post-Partition readjustments required by the economy'.[3] The commission's realistic assessment was tempered on pessimism: 'With all the effort that the First Five Year Plan will represent, it will be possible barely to restore by 1955–56 the pre-War standards of consumption in regard to essentials like food and cloth.'[4] The aims of the First Plan were thus modest:

a) First, to 'rectify the disequilibrium in the economy caused by the war and Partition'.

b) Second, to 'develop the basic resources necessary for making possible a rapid rate of economic development'.

c) And, finally, 'to organize in the fields of agriculture, cottage industries and large-scale industries such machinery as will permit the exercise of guidance and control over these activities by the public sector and public policy.'[5]

In overall terms, the First Plan ended up being 'more or less a public expenditure programme rather than a full-fledged national investment plan as such'.[6] This was not surprising, as much had gone wrong with the economic climate since the euphoric days of the Bombay Plan. Grappling with urgent economic problems, the official planners in New Delhi's Yojana Bhavan realized that the road to development was far tougher than envisaged. They had also become aware that much larger investments were needed and that any achievements would be smaller in magnitude than imagined. As 'Mr Planning' Tarlok Singh later reminisced: 'Now we know better. We have a fuller measure of the economic, social and organizational difficulties to be reckoned with. The problem of resources, both external and internal, and of economic policy generally, is better understood. The tasks ahead are far bigger than we realized.'[7]

Partition

Unleashing the biggest migration in human history in the midst of unprecedented communal violence and rioting, the economic impact of Partition had been nothing short of disastrous. In the final reckoning, more than 15 million people had been uprooted and an estimated 1 million had died.[8] Rehabilitating the refugees streaming in was the most urgent—and costly—task at hand. More than Rs 42 crore was spent on the current account on refugees in the first four years (until 1950–51) and Rs 20 crore on the capital account. Over 75 per cent of this expenditure was on immediate relief; the enormous expenses on resettlement would come only later.[9] The refugees were still 'consuming agents, not producing agents'.[10] Partition also led to food shortages of at least 1 million tons. So, despite the desperate dearth of foreign exchange, food imports were increased dramatically.[11] There were also shortages of various commodities, including those arising from the loss of cotton and jute growing areas to Pakistan. To make matters worse, before long, the Indian government's economic burden was accentuated by the outbreak of conflict in Kashmir.

Neither the political leadership nor the Bombay Planners, three of whom had been involved in some of the earliest studies to consider the economic impact of Partition, could anticipate the magnitude of the problems. One study on the possible economic impact of Partition had been conducted in 1944 by Matthai, together with Homi Mody, for the Sapru Committee on Constitutional Reforms. This study was later published independently as *A Memorandum on the Economic and Financial Aspects of Pakistan*.[12] Considering the fluidity of the political situation when they conducted their study,

Matthai and Mody visualized two possible scenarios. In the first, Partition would be carried out keeping intact the provincial boundaries, i.e. the Muslim-majority provinces would come together to form a new state. In the second scenario, boundaries would be redrawn on the basis of the contiguous Muslim-majority districts in Punjab and Bengal. Mody and Matthai concluded that Pakistan would be a viable economic unit if Partition was to occur province-wise. However, if the boundaries were to be drawn on the basis of Muslim-majority districts, the position of Pakistan would not be a happy one. They concluded that in both scenarios, the two independent states of India and Pakistan would need to cooperate in the spheres of economy and defence. In their view, a large free-trade zone would be essential for the future development of the two economies. They put forward the concept of the 'optimum economic unit', under which the two states would have minimum custom barriers and large-scale trade and exchange. If the goal was to raise the general standard of living, then there existed the need for effective cooperation between the two states. Without such cooperation, they predicted, Partition would be a recipe for economic disaster for both countries.

Ardeshir Dalal was the second Bombay Planner who had looked at the economic consequences of Partition. In his *An Alternative to Pakistan*, published in February 1943, he emphasized how difficult it would be for Pakistan's economy to function after separation from India, with it being cut off from the 'great economic and industrial future' which India may look forward to. He urged Hindus to make concessions to placate the Muslims and to keep the country united.

G.D. Birla too was concerned about the economic ramifications of India's division. In April 1947, *Eastern Economist*, a weekly publication owned by him, published a series of studies focused on the implications of Partition in terms of division of natural resources, budget allocations, distribution of industry and, not the least, the agrarian situation.[13] Based on these studies, the *Eastern Economist* concluded that there would be a major gap between the economic resources of India and Pakistan. It predicted that Pakistan would become a viable economic unit only after about a decade. Till then 'co-operation with the Indian Union on mutually advantageous terms is inescapable'.[14] In June 1947, Birla published *Basic Facts Relating to Hindustan and Pakistan*, which further explored the issue.[15] He prefaced his study with the bold statement that 'Hindu India' would be stronger than Pakistan. He advocated economic coordination between the two states and concluded that 'it would be in the interest of both the parts to put up co-ordinated efforts in order that the whole of India may be able to achieve high economic prosperity, strength and dignity'.[16] Thus, the view that there needed to be some sort of economic unity was one of the fundamental premises of the Bombay Planners.

However, all such hopes of economic cooperation between the two nascent nations were soon dashed, what with the bloodshed and bitterness that accompanied Partition. Just a few days before 15 August 1947, John

Matthai, then serving as member for industry and supply in the interim government, noted that he 'little realized' that Independence and Partition 'would bring in its wake such horrible consequences to the economy of the country'.[17]

What else went wrong

Quite apart from the economic crisis which accompanied Partition, there were existing public expenditure commitments in terms of development schemes which had been in place since the 1940s. These went back to the colonial government's early attempts at planning, most of which were in the areas of irrigation and power and included several large multipurpose river valley projects, including the Tungabhadra, Mahanadi, Damodar Valley, Kosi River and Rihand dam projects. Thus, when the government of independent India started its planning exercise in 1950, the task was not so much to draw up new plans as to bring 'order out of the chaos of existing public expenditure', as the economist V.K.R.V. Rao put it.[18] In the initial years, accordingly, the main brief of the newly founded Planning Commission was to concentrate on coordinating central programmes already in existence.

To aggravate matters, rampant post-war inflation was far 'more offensive' in its impact on the economy than even during the War.[19] Another matter of grave concern was a sharp decline in the industrial production index, from 120.0 in 1945–46 to 112.4 in February 1949.[20] Finally, the hopes that had been pinned on the sterling balance (*see Chapter 2*) as an invaluable funding source for post-war economic reconstruction were belied. Even before 1950, the sterling balance had been liquidated by more than 60 per cent, and the capital equipment that was expected to be bought from it did not materialize.[21]

Not surprisingly, India's first finance minister, John Matthai, grew deeply concerned at this situation. He realized that Partition 'has left the country not only with a disorganized but with a well-nigh shattered economy'. In his view, the task before the new government was 'not to recast our economic structure but to piece together their fragments into which it had broken and get it going again before reshaping it'.[22]

Disillusionment with the practice of planning

In such grim conditions, the First Five-Year Plan could be no more than a modest document.[23] Still, considering that its underlying philosophy, structure and approach were remarkably similar to those of the Bombay Plan, its publication brought much hope to its authors, and business persons generally 'felt beholden'.[24] Industry leaders enthusiastically pledged fulfilment of production targets set by the Plan. By early 1953, FICCI claimed that these had already been reached. However, despite the many similarities between the Bombay Plan and the First Five-Year Plan in structure and fundamental outlook, the way planning unfolded led to growing differences between business leaders and the establishment. These differences came out in the open in the mid-1950s.

When business leaders had supported the idea of controls and industrial licensing, they thought such measures would promote equitable economic progress and 'expected that the machinery for operation of controls and execution of public sector projects would be efficient and progressive'.[25] To their dismay, they were confronted with a plethora of controls, red tape and needless bureaucratic restrictions that mushroomed quickly. Industrial licensing, before anyone realized it, became as ubiquitous as it was byzantine. Decision-making within officialdom moved 'at a snail's pace', with files 'moving from ministry to ministry'.[26] Birla, one of the moving spirits behind the Bombay Plan, characterized officialdom as a 'dilatory, hide-bound' bureaucratic machinery.[27] To Thakurdas, all this was part of an alarming 'trend' of the government exercising 'increasing powers of regimentation'.[28] In the operation of controls which developed, there existed 'great woodenness and rigidity and a tendency to proliferate in a wholly unrealistic manner', contended H.V.R. Iyengar, governor of the Reserve Bank of India from 1957 to 1962. Controls acted as no less than 'brakes on production', and it was becoming clear that they were not even helping keep down prices.[29] As early as in 1951, business leaders were pleading for a reconsideration of controls. In the words of the FICCI president, these had become 'numerous, unwieldy and complicated', creating a situation where even the government and authorities were not clear about them.

'In such a situation, the difficulties of any business firm or a merchant, can well be imagined.'[30] Controls, lamented Shroff, 'have caught the community in such a maze of regulations that elaborate procedures have had to be set out with the result that progress is hampered'. Government rules like the Companies Act, in Shroff's view, became a 'masterpiece at preventing people from getting into joint-stock enterprises'. By the 1960s, such were the powers the bureaucracy had arrogated to itself that a mill Shroff was in charge of had to employ no less than sixteen clerks just to fill out forms and file returns![31] The proliferation of red tape led to despondency. As the economist and a former Reserve Bank of India governor I.G. Patel put it: 'Once introduced, each policy acquired its own momentum and vested interests and became difficult to limit, let alone reverse.'[32]

Increasingly, it was felt that the political leadership was showing itself to be 'doctrinaire' and lacking in 'realism'. This became amply evident in the mid-1950s with Nehru's escalating leftist pronouncements in the lead-up to the second general elections. In January 1955, at its annual session at Avadi, the Congress resolved that the 'socialist pattern of society' was its avowed objective. The leftists within the party even hoped to amend Article 31 of the Constitution, under which compensation for acquisition of private property by the state would become discretionary and non-justiciable. This called into question the basic right to own property. Alarmed, FICCI warned the Congress against amending the Constitution 'to suit the desires of the executive'.[33] Business leaders became increasingly edgy with the unfolding political situation. Although they realized that Nehru, after all, was not contemplating a socialist revolution or a wholesale scheme of 'nationalization', the signs were everywhere that private enterprise would not be given the voice in economic decision-making which they had hoped for. The Planning Commission decreed that all 'major decisions regarding production, distribution, consumption and investment— in fact, all socio-economic relationships—must be made by agencies informed of social purpose'. The public sector was now expected to grow 'not only absolutely but also relatively to the private sector'.[34] A series of policy measures further set the direction. In 1955, the Imperial Bank was nationalized, as was the life insurance sector. A new Industrial Policy Resolution adopted in 1956 substantially increased the number of industries reserved for the public sector. It also did away with the ten-year guarantee against nationalization of existing enterprises which a previous resolution had promised. Such was the zeitgeist preceding the Second Five-Year Plan that it marked the real point of departure between the views of the Bombay Plan authors and those of the government.

Although there remained some similarity between the underlying philosophy of the Bombay Plan and the official beliefs embodied in the Second Five-Year Plan and the Industrial Policy Resolution, both these policy documents remained open-ended and allowed for large discretion which, in potential terms, meant a tilt towards the public sector and, by implication, a deliberate marginalization of the private sector.[35] Political observers openly talked about the curious ambiguity in Nehru's rhetoric, as nobody quite knew what his 'socialist pattern of society' meant. Birla's *Eastern Economist* characterized the situation as one marked by 'stringent control as well as complete decontrol, restriction of private enterprise and assistance to private enterprise and increasing nationalization and decreasing nationalization'.[36] Business leaders wondered what purpose would be served by 'unsettling the minds of industrialists time and again by throwing such bombshells'.[37]

The growing divergence, even conflict, between the public and private sectors came to feature in the political rhetoric. A disheartened Birla told Congress heavyweight and then Union Home Minister G.B. Pant: 'The British have gone and the princes and zamindars are in the background. The Congress, accustomed to a target for its hatred, is now finding only one target—that is the capitalist.'[38] The mid-1950s thus were a time of much disquiet for business. At the FICCI annual session, Mody warned the government not to take measures that would mean 'we will have to be carried in an ambulance'. Many business leaders, especially from Bombay, perturbed by the drift in official policies, saw the need for lobbying and mobilizing to effect 'speedy action whenever an issue arises'. They came together by forming a small and relatively manageable organization, the Council of Industry, which included in its committee four authors of the Bombay Plan—J.R.D. Tata, Lala Sri Ram, Kasturbhai Lalbhai and Birla.[39]

In the lead-up to the Second Five-Year Plan, business leaders, especially Lalbhai and Birla, worked closely with their peers to posit a vigorous rebuttal to its premises. They questioned the overall plan size and argued that its targets were 'utterly beyond the resources of the country'. Such targets, they argued, could only be implemented after imposing high taxes and drastic controls over consumption, with the government 'deficit running into a figure greatly beyond the margin of safety'.[40] Birla's *Eastern Economist* denounced P.C. Mahalanobis, the moving spirit behind the Second Plan, as a 'statistician completely devoid of a sense of economic organization'. It described his Plan's framework as no more than a 'theoretical shibboleth which, if enforced, would in one sweep endanger India's future industrialization'.[41] In the view of business captains, Mahalanobis's plan ignored the basic economic criterion of efficiency and performance in favouring the public sector over the more competitive private sector. Further, they contended, the foreign exchange needed to finance the Plan had been grossly underestimated.[42] Business planners took every opportunity to warn T.T. Krishnamachari, the finance minister, other Cabinet ministers and even the prime minister himself that it would be 'simply impossible' to implement the Plan without a substantial injection of foreign exchange. The heavy import requirements of the Plan, it was feared, would trigger a foreign exchange crisis. Birla cautioned that the economy would soon be on the brink of a crisis that would upset the whole 'apple-cart'.[43] Birla went so far as to call the Mahalanobis model dangerous in its propensity to 'ignore realities and base our hopes on mistaken calculations and emotional approaches'. He urged New Delhi to stop 'toying with ideas likely to take us on a backward march'.[44]

Although Birla and the other business leaders had strongly supported the idea of a planned, developmental state, as evinced in their authorship of the Bombay Plan, in a cruel irony, the process of official planning, as it unfolded, deeply disappointed them. They worried that they faced the 'pre-emption, rather than prohibition, of private entrepreneurship over an increasing area of industry through state enterprise'. What the businessmen planners had hoped for was some sort of creative partnership between the state and the market, in keeping with Keynes's dictum that planned development is the 'more efficient' alternative. They had wanted government direction, planning and regulation that would affect investment decisions, no doubt, but they wanted that the functioning of the market should continue alongside. In many ways, what they were hoping for was possibly the kind of cooperation between the state and the private sector which came to be realized in many East Asian countries in the 1960s and 1970s, to remarkable success. After all, 'private enterprise and the Congress were allies in the fight for independence'. But 'when the fight was won and the time came for the coronation, the Congress, to the Federation's dismay, put the industrial crown on its own head'.[45]

'From the High Noon of the Bombay Plan to the Wintry Despair of 1960'

Considering their disillusionment, it is unsurprising that business leaders began to think of ways of coming together to deal with the challenge. On 12 January 1954, a decade after the publication of the Bombay Plan, an important meeting took place again in Bombay. It was convened by Mody, a director of Tata Sons, and the cost of hosting it was borne by JRD and Birla.[46] As many as twenty-nine business captains were present to discuss the grave situation 'confronting industrial interest and to formulate a plan of action' to 'save the private sector from the dangers which are gathering around it'.[47] The attendees included five of the Bombay Planners: Purshottamdas Thakurdas, Kasturbhai Lalbhai, J.R.D. Tata, Lala Shri Ram and A.D. Shroff. Birla could not be personally present, but the meeting had his 'fullest support' and he granted Mody the right to be his proxy.[48] An extensive discussion took place on 'legislative and administrative acts' of the government, on 'the burdens being piled on industry' and on 'the interference in the operations of industry by the government'. Business leaders boldly criticized the government for the manner in which private enterprise was being 'hamstrung'. They emphasized that a mixed economy could only work if there was 'co-existence of state and free enterprise', if they were 'equal and autonomous forces' and worked towards 'supplementing and fortifying each other'.[49] To deal with the challenges confronting private enterprise, they decided to set up a small committee to be called 'Council of Industry' for taking 'speedy action when any issues effecting commercial life arose'. Four of the Bombay planners— Birla, JRD, Shri Ram and Kasturbhai—were members of this council, along with seven other industrialists.[50]

The sombre backdrop to the 1954 meeting was in stark contrast to the euphoric atmosphere of a decade earlier, in January 1944, when the Bombay Plan was drawn up. The optimism which had then marked the business leaders' expectations for the nation's tryst with prosperity had given way to a deep sense of frustration and disillusionment. In the decade since the publication of the Bombay Plan, the Planners felt that much had changed for the worse. Issues such as excessive regulation of the private sector, the pervasiveness of official controls, burgeoning corruption in the bureaucracy and the growing political rhetoric against private enterprise had all become matters of concern. In addition, from time to time, the government took up deleterious policies towards specific sectors. By the mid-1950s, there existed a real gulf between the business leaders who had drafted the Bombay Plan and the government.

Revisiting the Bombay Plan authors

As noted in Chapter 6, the one individual among the Planners who had gained official recognition was Ardeshir Dalal. After Part I of the Bombay Plan was published, he had been invited to join the viceroy's executive council and given charge of the newly created department of planning and development. Excited at the prospect of helping in the official planning endeavour, Dalal made much effort to energize the process of planning which was being initiated by the colonial government. He urged provincial governments to submit post-war reconstruction plans and appointed several committees to look into proposed projects, among other things. The several hurdles confronting him, however, led him to conclude that the colonial government's efforts were not entirely sincere. It ended up as a disappointing experience for Dalal, who spent less than two years in the job. He resigned and returned to Tata Sons in January 1946, resuming his position as partner and director of TISCO.[51]

Of the Bombay Plan authors, it was Matthai who ended up having the most illustrious innings in public service, although he too ended up disillusioned. In September 1946, at the invitation of Nehru, Matthai took leave from Tata Sons to join the interim government. He was independent India's first minister of railways till September 1948, after which he was appointed finance minister and he presented two annual budgets. Although it seemed as if Matthai was having a good run in office, in reality he was slowly getting disheartened and taking steps to distance himself from the corridors of power, and by 1950, he had resigned from government.

Ironically, it was the issue of economic planning on which he came to have serious differences with the prime minister. Although both Matthai and Nehru shared a deep interest in planning,[52] since assuming office as finance minister, Matthai had begun to reconsider his ideas about putting in place five-year plans. With an insider's view, he could see how dramatically the economic scenario had changed from the days of the Bombay Plan. He blamed the Partition and the 'damage it did to every segment' of life for the unsettled and bleak state of the economy. This convinced him that it was premature to undertake plans on a large scale. There were already plans to the tune of nearly Rs 3000 crore dating back to 1945–46, from the time of the colonial government. These had been put on hold for lack of finances, technical expertise and material. He felt that plans needed to be prioritized, based on the 'real resources' available. He came to believe that five-year plans could 'only be carried out by budgeting for larger deficits, which is unthinkable in the present circumstances'.[53] As finance minister, he made the case that the 'general scarcity of money and materials made it difficult to implement any new plans'. He also believed that in the aftermath of Partition, 'conditions were so fluid that no data of any permanent value could be collected'. Hence, 'there was just not enough data to put forth plan projections'.

Matthai and Nehru 'had many long arguments' on the wisdom of launching centralized planning in such difficult conditions. However, Nehru was determined to have his way. Thus, in March 1950, a national Planning Commission was set up. Matthai attributed the prime minister's stubbornness on the formation of the commission to 'political expediency'. Rueful that the prime minister 'in his approach to the problems of government laid more emphasis on formulating a programme for the future than on providing solutions for immediate difficulties', Matthai began to feel that Nehru was 'following the instinct of the true politician rather than the man of affairs intent on fulfilling the job at hand'.[54] The jostling in New Delhi's corridors of power disillusioned the economist in Matthai.

As the Planning Commission's influence expanded and it began exercising powers which clashed with the jurisdiction of the finance and other such ministries, Matthai became even more dissatisfied with the government's functioning.[55] Given the commission's 'ever-growing influence' and the fact that its members even attended Cabinet meetings, Matthai found that it was near impossible to take a position contrary to it. He contended that the Planning Commission had become a 'parallel Cabinet', as a result of which 'Cabinet responsibility had definitely weakened', and warned that the commission's increasing influence would 'weaken' the authority of the finance ministry and 'gradually reduce the Cabinet to practically a registering body'.[56] Extremely upset, Matthai insisted on resigning as finance minister, despite much persuasion by Nehru to the contrary. A saddened Matthai later reminisced: 'Hence it was that the Bombay Planner lost his interest for the time being in planning and the reformist of 1947 was more interested in conserving than in redesigning the structure of Indian economy'.[57]

Like Dalal, Matthai returned to the comforting fold of the Tatas after his resignation from the Cabinet. His disappointment with the ways of ruling politicians and his eagerness to contribute to public life led him to stand for parliamentary elections in 1952 as an independent candidate from Kottayam constituency in Kerala. However, he was forced to withdraw his nomination papers because the Congress candidate challenged his nomination on the ground that he was a Tata employee.[58] He then took over charge of the steel business from Dalal as vice chairman of Tata Steel. He was to spend the next nine years at Bombay House, the Tata group's corporate headquarters. He enjoyed these years, especially his lunches with JRD and Mody, who fondly called him 'Brother-John' and 'Brother-Praise-the Lord John'.[59] In 1955, he was invited to serve as vice chancellor of Bombay University and in 1958 as vice chancellor of Kerala University.

Ardeshir Shroff, Matthai's colleague at Bombay House, had, over the years, also become a vociferous critic of the Nehru government's economic policies. He now played a key role in galvanizing businesspersons to speak out against the government's 'suspicion and irrelevant ideologies' that were bound to 'produce disastrous consequences in the economy of the country'. He lost no occasion to warn business interests that if they did not come together, their cause would be 'lost by default'.[60] Unlike Matthai, Shroff's criticism sprang not from any opposition to the timing of the official five-year plans but from the planning as it was being practised in India. Although still convinced of the need for planning and its role in reducing economic inequality and ensuring social justice, and the need for having in place controls over private enterprise, Shroff expected that such controls and the execution of public-sector projects must be 'efficient and progressive', which he did not find to be so in practice. The growing restrictions being clamped on private enterprise and the rapid expansion of the public sector, despite its all too apparent inefficiencies, disillusioned him. The political leadership's anti-business rhetoric, its lack of realism and its 'slackness in political standard', all made him lose faith in the official machinery.[61]

Finally, in July 1956, Shroff, along with Murarji Vaidya of the All-India Manufacturers Association and Minoo Masani, author of the popular version of the Bombay Plan, launched the Forum of Free Enterprise. The forum promised to be a non-partisan, non-political organization committed to bringing to 'public notice the achievements of free enterprise . . . and the manner in which it can make its contribution to the economic development of India in order to raise the standard of living.'[62] The forum, however, did not stand for unbridled laissez faire,[63] and supported the state's role in planning while simultaneously warning against pervasive government controls and too large a role for the public sector, as such policies were destroying private economic initiative in the Hayekian sense.[64]

In 1959, the Forum of Free Enterprise, along with the All India Agriculturists Federation, helped do the groundwork that led to the formation of the right-wing Swatantra Party, which emerged as a leading opposition party to the Congress. On a personal front, Shroff continued to serve as a director at Tata Sons and also taught part-time at his alma mater, Sydenham College, in Bombay. Within the Tatas, he worked to revive the group's textile ventures while continuing his old role of financial and stock market advisory on behalf of Tata Sons. He had also played a key role in building up the New India Assurance Corporation, a Tata enterprise, which was nationalized in 1956, along with other life insurance firms, much to his chagrin.

Though Shroff's sentiments of despair were shared by the authors of the Bombay Plan, none of them joined the Forum of Free Enterprise. Shri Ram went to the extent of opposing its formation. He saw no wisdom in businesspersons openly voicing their opposition to the government. In his view, 'the more we shout about private sector and public sector, the more we educate unsympathetic people and [the] more enemies we make'. He even wanted FICCI to pass a 'resolution requesting their member-bodies and members not to make too much noise or have a body like the Forum of Free Enterprise' which, he argued, 'unnecessarily, in my opinion, antagonizes even good friends'.[65] Though he was against the forum's formation, Shri Ram remained a vocal critic of the government's economic policies within FICCI. He urged the political leadership not to let businessmen down after they had 'played their part in getting independence'. Traders and commercial classes, he argued, are 'also the brains of the country. It is this class that is in the distribution trade which purchases most of the goods made by Indian industry.' Distribution channels had 'taken ages to evolve and develop' which, he alleged, were being destroyed by official controls.[66]

Thakurdas too felt himself to be quite out of tune with government policies. In protest against government interference, Thakurdas resigned from two of the foremost organizations with which he had been involved through much of his public career—the East India Cotton Association and the Reserve Bank of India. Resignation from the East India Cotton Association, believed Thakurdas, seemed to be the only honourable course, given the way the Government of India's textile policy was unfolding. The state of the cotton industry was a matter of much concern following Partition, as most of the cotton-growing areas had gone to Pakistan. As a result, there occurred a sharp decline in the supply of raw cotton and, for the first time in half a century, India had to resort to imports, which cost the exchequer the hefty sum of Rs 64.23 crore in just one year, 1948–49. Rather than trying to tackle the shortfall caused by Partition, Thakurdas and other mill owners complained, the government's own policies were making matters worse. These included diverting 8 million acres of land from cotton to groundnut production on the pretext of food shortage,[67] and official controls and price ceilings that were rendering Indian textiles uncompetitive. Together with Kasturbhai, Shri Ram and Birla, Thakurdas vehemently protested against the textile policy. In 1952, he warned the political leadership of the 'definite disservice' they were doing to the industry and for being 'most short-sighted . . . if the textile industry is to be artificially put back or rather pushed back'. Thakurdas argued that it had taken India half a century to emerge as a 'respectable competitor' to Lancashire in England and other countries in terms of quality and the output of piece goods. He saw state policies as 'self-defeating in their nature as sooner or later a crisis is bound to overtake the textile industry, owing partly to world conditions and partly owing to the increasing imports heaped upon it'.[68]

Kasturbhai similarly argued that 'there could not be a greater paradox than the fact that our national leaders, who fought the British for the removal of the excise duty on cotton cloth which stood at three and a half per cent . . . are coming forward to levy a duty which is about six and a quarter per cent, at the present level of prices.'[69] Even a normally cautious Shri Ram openly criticized the political leadership for its 'contradictory policies which on the one hand asked mills to reduce their prices complaining that they were undercutting handlooms and on the other hand objected to mills being closed down.'[70]

The final straw for Thakurdas came in 1956 when the central government quite abruptly asked the East India Cotton Association to impose a new price ceiling 'for the season' on cotton.[71] This was far below the official price ceiling that was already in place.[72] In Thakurdas's view, this denied the cotton grower a 'secure fair price, in accordance with the forces of demand and supply . . . even within the limitations of the official ceiling prices'. In a show of protest, Thakurdas resigned as chairman and director of the East India Cotton Association's board. He rued that he had been able to fight the colonial powers to preserve the independence of the cotton trade, 'but I cannot fight our government, nor do I seem to be able at this juncture to carry them with me'. His resignation letter went on to state: 'The trend of recent developments is for the authorities to exercise increasing powers of regimentation and for the business community to yield to them.'[73] This marked the end of a long and much cherished relationship for Thakurdas. Ironically, barely two years before, in June 1954, the association had lavishly celebrated the diamond jubilee of Thakurdas's involvement with it by installing his statue at the Cotton Green building in Bombay.[74] The statue had been unveiled by no less a person than senior Congress leader and then chief minister of Bombay, Morarji Desai.[75]

Thakurdas went a step further by also ending his twenty-year relationship with the Reserve Bank of India. A director on its central board since its inception, Thakurdas refused to be renominated to the board in 1957 in protest against the finance minister T.T. Krishnamachari's interference in the bank's functioning. Thakurdas made his indignation publicly known. The 'happenings in the last couple of weeks in relation between the board of the Reserve Bank and the central finance ministry are so extraordinary, one-sided and unprovoked that I felt that it is not to the interest of the country that any non-official should avoidably keep up his connection with the Reserve Bank,' declared Thakurdas.[76]

In Ahmedabad, Kasturbhai took up cudgels on behalf of commercial interests on a range of issues. For instance, when the Bombay government proposed its levy of multipoint sales tax, Kasturbhai supported traders in Maharashtra and Gujarat who were against it. So annoyed was he that he led a 50,000-strong protest march from Maneck Chowk to Premabhai Hall in Ahmedabad, which was accompanied by a hartal. At a public rally, Kasturbhai gave a strong speech criticizing the government for its 'steam-roller' methods.[77] He also became active in the Maha Gujarat movement and served as president of the Maha Gujarat Sima Samiti (boundary committee) demanding formation of a separate state of Gujarat consisting of the Gujarati districts of the Bombay state, Saurashtra and Kutch.[78]

Like the other authors of the Bombay Plan, JRD too was feeling alienated by the official policies and their 'potential danger of concentrating economic power in the hands of a small politician-cum-bureaucratic minority'.[79] Despite his familial relations with the prime minister, JRD found himself 'increasingly out of tune with him once he came to power'. It appeared to him that Nehru was conscious of their mutual disagreements on economic policy. Thus, once Nehru became prime minister, 'our contacts, while always warm became increasingly infrequent'.[80] Admitting that he shared 'Jawaharlal's deep sympathy for the poor and deep urge to alleviate their poverty', JRD said: '[Yet] I was denied, or denied myself opportunities to help him in that task by my disagreement with his socialism.'[81] It was almost as though Nehru deliberately avoided discussions. He 'always looked out of the window or asked me to look at the panda in the garden whenever I wanted to talk seriously about the economy', JRD later recalled.[82] Harbouring 'tremendous dreams and expectations of cooperation between the private sector and the Government', JRD admitted later that his 'one sorrow and regret is that the government had, from Jawaharlal Nehru onwards . . . not allowed many of us imbued with enthusiasm and hope to do enough'.[83] A saddened JRD reminisced afterwards: 'My life has been a struggle—never once has any prime minister asked me what I thought of the economic policy of the country. In no other country would this have happened.'[84]

Compared with his colleagues, Birla had a more nuanced view of the unfolding political situation. Though he too was openly critical of the 'reckless' turn the political leadership was taking, he was not unduly perturbed. Based on his long experience, he understood that in a democratic set-up, radical pronouncements were watered down in the process of debate and discussion before they became policy. Further, in a democracy, business could not be ignored. Thus, when nervous colleagues asked him to lead a deputation to the prime minister in the build-up to the Second Five-Year Plan, Birla wisely advised that the first step was to 'prepare' the mind of ministers in charge of commerce, industry and finance. Only on receiving their 'blessings' should the prime minister be approached.[85] He did meet with Nehru when the need arose. Thus, in March 1955, he and Kasturbhai expressed their concerns to the prime minister on day-to-day issues and requested for informal ways to resolve differences between business and government. They proposed an ad hoc committee of the Cabinet that could meet with businesspersons, more dialogue between business and government agencies, and regular informal meetings with the prime minister himself. Birla and Kasturbhai met Nehru again a few months later, in January 1956, together with other businesspersons, and took up these issues. Whenever important matters arose, Birla wrote to Nehru and also corresponded with Morarji Desai and T.T. Krishnamachari, critiquing the draft proposal of the Second Five-Year Plan. Birla warned the political leadership that the economy could soon be in crisis. He urged the government to stop 'toying with ideas likely to take us on a backward march'.[86] These were strong words, and they were coming from Birla who, with his astute understanding of the workings and limits of Nehruvian socialism, had always been cautious about not alienating the top leadership. Birla's protégé, P.S. Lokanathan, had much earlier distanced himself from economic developments in the country, opting instead to become executive secretary to the United Nations Economic Commission of Asia and the Far East, in which position he served from 1947 to 1956.

At a personal level, the other Bombay Plan authors continued to serve on official committees whenever they were called upon to do so. Thus, Matthai headed the taxation enquiry committee in 1953, Shroff chaired the railways supplies enquiry committee, and Kasturbhai played a consultative role in the economic committee of the ministry of finance. Kasturbhai and Birla remained active in many government initiatives and helped with fund-raising for varied causes.[87] Yet, they did not play the role they had expected to play in independent India's economic policy-making. What Iyengar had said about Dalal tragically held true for all the Bombay Planners: they had moved 'from the high noon of the Bombay Plan to the wintry despair of 1960'.[88]

Legacy of the Bombay Plan

Individually, the Bombay Planners may have been marginalized in the planning process of independent India and suffered personal disappointments. Yet, few would contest that in many aspects their influence as a body was all too visible in India's official planning endeavour which saw the formulation of twelve Five-Year Plans from 1951 till 2014, when the Planning Commission was abolished by the newly-elected Bharatiya Janata Party government.[89] Through these six decades, the Bombay Plan served as a reference point for all these plans. There seems little difference between the basic approach of the Bombay Plan and the approach of the Planning Commission of the Government of India and it would by no means be far-fetched to say that the Planning Commission actually got its inspiration from the Bombay Plan . . . It was all there in the Bombay Plan—the concept of massive state intervention in the economy, of a mixed private and public sector enterprise, the emphasis on heavy industry, the need for foreign capital and the need for deficit financing,' asserted Iyengar.[90]

While several similarities in the underlying philosophy and approach are clearly evident, and it would be fair to assert that independent India's Five-Year Plans gained inspiration from and drew upon the ideas of the Bombay Plan, the most significant legacy of the Bombay Plan, by far, lies in its legitimizing the very idea of planning.[91]

Both the Bombay Planners and the official planners shared the same premise—that state intervention and planning were prerequisites for the nation's long-term development, since this alone could bring about the structural changes so critically needed to pull India out of its economic backwardness. Consequently, the unrestricted operation of market forces was frowned upon. The Bombay Plan architects, although industrialists or business executives themselves, accepted the notion that India's existing economic structure, based on private enterprise and ownership, had failed to bring about a satisfactory distribution of national income. To ameliorate this, they believed it was crucial to 'bring in' the state, though only after independence from colonial rule had been secured. They took a progressive view of the state, expressing the hope that it 'should exercise in the interests of the community a considerable measure of intervention and control'.[92] An 'enlargement of the positive as well as preventive functions of the state is essential', they argued, for any large-scale economic planning. 'This is inherent in the idea of planning and its implications must be fully admitted.'[93] Since they recognized the need for a strong state to effect structural transformation and alleviate poverty, they expected the state to be the central economic actor in the initial fifteen years which were envisaged as the period of intensive planning.

In a similar spirit, successive Five-Year Plans formulated by the Planning Commission also placed their faith in a strong state whose intervention was regarded as essential for developmental planning. Accordingly, the state came to be charged with defining the economic strategy, allocating resources, carrying out the necessary investments in infrastructure and basic industry and, not the least, charting the path for private capital and regulating its operations. The Industries (Development and Regulation) Act of 1951 ruled that neither new industrial units nor expansion of existing ones could take place without a license from the central government. Such a regulation echoed the ideas of the authors of the Bombay Plan. From the Second Five-Year Plan onwards, the state became even more central in national plans as it appropriated for itself the role of producer and regulator. The Planning Commission advocated 'large planning' and investment in 'capital goods to produce capital goods', to be implemented through the state's centralized industrial investment planning.[94] Thus, insofar as espousal of the state's central role in the economy is concerned, the views of the Bombay Plan authors and national planners were strikingly alike. In a structural sense, therefore, the official Five-Year Plans were the offspring of the Bombay Plan. A.K. Dasgupta, one of India's pioneering development economists, observed that it was from the Bombay Plan that the official plans derived their 'formulation of a growth target, the application of the concept of the capital-output ratio towards an assessment of the investment need'.[95]

Both the Bombay Plan and the Five-Year Plans subscribed to the concept of a 'mixed economy'. Although the Bombay Plan assured private enterprise a key role, its mission of reducing gross inequalities required decentralizing ownership of the means of production. For this reason, the authors of the Bombay Plan suggested that the state should control, own and manage public utilities and basic industries. The outline of the Five-Year Plans, as they evolved in the 1950s and 1960s, came to be considerably shaped by these ideas. This is most evident in the Planning Commission's framework of a 'mixed economy', in which the state and private enterprise were seen as having complementary roles. Material resources, it was agreed, should be distributed in such a way that it would 'subserve the common good', and the Five-Year Plans were expected to disallow a concentration of wealth or means of production, as such concentration or monopoly was seen to be to the 'common detriment'.[96]

In keeping with this spirit, the Industrial Policy Resolution of 1956 divided industries into three groups. In the first group, 'Schedule A', future development in sectors such as railways, air transport, arms, ammunition and atomic energy was left to the state, either independently or jointly with the private sector. In 'Schedule B', the second group, the government was to take the initiative in sectors such as machine tools, fertilizers, synthetic rubber, road and sea transport, but existing private firms would be allowed to continue their operations. It was only in the third group, 'Schedule C', that the field was left open to private enterprise. Although the 'commanding heights' of the economy were occupied by the state, thanks to its ownership and control of all basic and capital goods industries, the division between the public and private sectors in developing other industries was not rigid. The Second Five-Year Plan, while increasing the role of the public sector, acknowledged the interdependence of the public and the private sectors, and stated that 'the Plan as a whole can go through only on the basis of simultaneous and balanced development in both sectors'.[97]

Another key similarity between the Bombay Plan and national Five-Year Plans is seen in the common emphasis on heavy or basic industry. For the authors of the Bombay Plan, basic industry was 'essential' for economic transformation, and they recognized that this must be developed rapidly. Basic industry was defined as generation of electric power, mining and metallurgy, engineering, chemicals, armaments, transport and cement. In the initial stages, the Bombay Plan authors wanted attention to be directed primarily towards industries involved in the production of power and capital goods. This, it was hoped, would accelerate the pace of industrialization, as it was the basic industries on which ultimately the whole economic development of the country was dependent. The Bombay Plan allocated more investment to heavy or basic industry, in percentage terms, than either the Second or the Third Plans. The communist leader E.M.S. Namboodiripad calculated, after taking into account the rise in prices, that the first three Five-Year Plans set aside only 33 per cent for industry, which was 'even less than the investments for basic industry' in the Bombay Plan, which had earmarked 44.8 per cent for industry.[98] Nevertheless, the doyens of the Planning Commission were equally conscious of the need for rapid industrialization. The First Plan emphasized increased industrial production and the Second Plan, even more than its predecessor, advocated 'large planning' and justified increased investment in machine-building and other capital goods industries to maximize long-term growth.

The similarity between the Bombay Plan and the Five-Year Plans extended to other avowed objectives too. The Bombay Plan authors had boldly defined the central problem as 'securing a general standard of living which would leave a reasonable margin over the minimum requirement of human life'.[99] This was precisely what independent India's national planners sought to do as well. The Cabinet resolution of 15 March 1950, which established the Planning Commission, declared that the objective of planning was to ensure that all citizens 'equally have the right to an adequate means of livelihood'.[100] Although both the Bombay Plan and the later Five-Year Plans acknowledged that agriculture would remain the predominant sector, the Bombay Plan had been more optimistic about reducing the share of agriculture in the national income.

The Bombay Plan, as noted in Chapter 5, was far more ambitious than the official Five-Year Plans and aimed at doubling per capita income within a fifteen-year span.

The First Five-Year Plan (1951–56), on the other hand, had a long-term perspective of doubling per capita income only over twenty-seven years. Where the Bombay Plan was truly pioneering was in its concern about reducing income inequality. It was not until the Third Five-Year Plan that the government recognized that measures were needed to radically reduce income disparities. As the Planning Commission veteran Tarlok Singh pointed out: 'Only in the Third Plan, and that too with some measure of caution, has the view been advanced that as a first step towards equality of opportunity for every citizen, the basic necessities must be provided for.'[101]

In another key respect, independent India's national plans followed the Bombay Plan, which was a 'trailblazer' in its espousal of deficit financing. Orthodox financial theories believed in balanced budgets, which meant that public expenditure be limited to current revenue, except during contingencies. The interwar years changed this view. There was a growing acceptance of the idea that budgetary deficits, or governments spending more than their revenues, were necessary to boost demand. With Keynes's theory of involuntary unemployment and his prescription of public investment with a budgetary deficit as a stimulant, this view gained further respectability. In India, the Bombay Planners were pioneers in advocating the concept of deficit financing, which was described as 'created money'. More than one-third of the Bombay Plan investment for the purpose of developmental planning, an estimated Rs 3400 crore, was to come from 'created money'. The principle of deficit financing came to be embraced by national planners too. 'The Planning Commission has since taken it over,' noted Dasgupta, and accepted deficit financing as 'one of the permissible ways of mobilizing domestic resources for economic development'.[102] Initially, deficit financing was used hesitantly. The First Five-Year Plan limited it to the release of sterling balances only when foreign assistance fell short. The Second Five-Year Plan more fully recognized the value of deficit financing in reducing unemployment, and the principle increasingly became indispensable to all planning efforts thereafter.[103]

Another point of convergence between the Bombay Plan and the official plans was the pessimism they shared over India's export prospects. One reason for this could be that during the 1940s and 1950s, there was no historical precedent of export-led growth in any part of the developing world. It was only much later, in the 1960s and 1970s, that the East Asian economies embarked on their export-led path of growth.

Despite the several striking similarities between the ideas of the Bombay Plan and the national plans, there were also important differences. One crucial difference was that the Bombay Plan expected the state to play an especially interventionist role in the initial fifteen-year period of intensive planning. Ironically, the Bombay Plan, which was the handiwork of Indian business, contemplated a larger role for the state than the First Five-Year Plan did. A central feature of the Bombay Plan was the comprehensive operation of controls in the spheres of production, distribution and pricing, prescription of work conditions and wages for labour, investment, and trade. Without such controls, it felt, economic development would hardly be possible. But it advocated that these controls should be discontinued after the initial fifteen-year window. Thereafter, as Chapter 5 has shown, the business leaders imagined that the role of the state would be limited to macroeconomic management of the economy.

In contrast to this, however, once official planning came to be entrenched by the 1960s, the bureaucracy increased its grip through an almost byzantine maze of controls. During the 1950s and 1960s, the balance kept steadily tilting towards the public sector, which began developing a stranglehold over key sectors of the economy. This was accompanied by a deep suspicion of private enterprise, and by the end of the 1960s, the chasm between the public and private sectors seemed unbridgeable.

ACKNOWLEDGEMENTS

Reconstructing the story of the Bombay Plan has taken much longer than it took its authors to write their manifesto. In these years, I have incurred many debts.

I must start with thanking Gurcharan Das for convincing me to work on the Bombay Plan and for the many discussions we have had and for being so encouraging throughout. I greatly enjoyed the many discussions I had with him and Bunu Das.

The generosity of many persons and institutions made this work possible. I thank my teachers—the late Anthony Low and Chris Bayly—most warmly for their encouragement while the book was in its early stages. I must also thank Judith Brown for always being so supportive. Parts of the book have been read by Dwijendra Tripathi, Susan Bayly, Thomas Timberg, Gita Piramal and Chikayoshi Nomura, and I thank them all for their comments and suggestions. Professor Dwijendra Tripathi, the doyen among Indian business historians, has always been most encouraging of my endeavours, and his passing away is a great loss to me. I am also grateful to Walter Friedman and Geoffrey Jones, the editors of the *Business History Review*, and two anonymous reviewers to whom some of the early ideas were presented for their comments. Thanks are also due to Tirthankar Roy, Robin Jeffrey and Aditya Mukherjee for their encouragement.

Many others have, over the years, provided help and support. I am most grateful to Basant Kumar Birla and the late Sarala Birla for their encouragement and cooperation. They opened up access to the G.D. Birla Papers which proved invaluable for this work. I also warmly thank Manjushree Khaitan for her keen interest in my work.

The archivists and librarians of a number of institutions facilitated this research, and I am very grateful to them. In Delhi, I would like to thank the staff at Mangalam, Nehru Memorial Museum and Library and the National Archives of India. In Pune, the archivist at Tata Central Archives, Rajendra Prasad Narla, was most helpful. The central libraries at the National University of Singapore (NUS) and Osaka University facilitated this research. I would also like to thank the India Office Records and Private Papers. Some of the ideas in this work were presented at a seminar at the University of Tokyo. Nita Mukherjee too shared valuable material with me about which I was earlier unaware. The illustrations in the book have been adapted from C.H.G. Moorehouse's drawings in Minoo Masani's *Picture of a Plan* (Oxford University Press, 1945).

I would also like to thank my colleagues at the history department of the NUS for their support through these years, especially Ian Gordon, Donna Brunero and, not least, Bruce Lockhart.

Among friends, there are many who need to be thanked. In Singapore, I thank Tai Yong, Sylvia Tan, Lily Kong, Vineeta Sinha, Manjusha Nair and Rahul Mukherjee. In Delhi, I thank Neerja and Hulas Singh, Salil Misra and Vijayshree for always being such good friends. Thanks also to Riho Isaka, Sumita Kale, Poonam Agarwal, Nalini Gupta and Manjriri Kamat for their support over the years. Many thanks are due to Amrita Varma for looking so carefully at the many drafts, for her incisive inputs and for her friendship.

My editors at Penguin, especially Milee Ashwarya and Lohit Jagwani, were very supportive and tolerant with my delayed submissions. I am most thankful to Shanuj V.C. for his meticulous editing of the book. Genevieve Chia and Khush Hal Lagdhiyan were most helpful at different phases while I was in search of research material.

My family has, as always, been most supportive and understanding. It is a pleasure to thank my mother; Anu and Kamal, Kapila and Anil, Ritu and Nitin, and Geeta for always allowing me to make their homes my own and for all they have done for me over the years. The younger generation has also always been most caring, and I thank Yasmin, Ayesha, Bhavna, Surbhi, Tarini and, of course, Archit. Taramani managed the house through the writing of this book and I thank her for this. Gyanesh and Vrinda have been invaluable sources of strength; they were tolerant of my research trips, and without their support this work would not have been possible.

Most of all, I would like to thank my Gurujans without whose blessings none of this would have been possible.

NOTES

Preface

1. Part I was published in January 1944, and Part II in December 1944. The two parts of the Plan were published as a Penguin Special in 1945. A popular version, *Picture of a Plan,* was written by Minoo Masani and illustrated by C.H.G. Moorhouse (November 1945).

2. Overseas too, businesspersons were formulating economic plans for implementation in their respective countries after the War ended. In the UK, the Federation of British Industries put forth its plan for reconstruction (see *Reconstruction: A Report of the Federation of British Industries,* 1942), as did several business organizations in the US (see Witham, *The Rise of the Corporate Moderates*). Individual corporations too got into the act. For instance, Unilever and its founders, the Lever brothers, published their ideas on the contours of the post-war economy (*The Problem of Unemployment*).

3. For an understanding of development ideas that were being debated in India, see Zachariah, *Developing India.*

On the Bombay Plan, see Sanyal, 'The Curious Case of the Bombay Plan'; Chattopadhyay, 'Attitude of Indian Business towards Economic Planning'; Chibber, *Locked in Place*; Lockwood, 'Was the Bombay Plan a Capitalist Plot?', pp. 99–116.

Chapter I: Indian Business Comes of Age: The World War II Years

1. *Times of India*, 1 March 1940.
2. See Kudaisya, *Life and Times of G.D. Birla*, Chapter 8: 'The War Years'.
3. Ibid.
4. Aggarwal, *History of the Supply Department*, p. 1.
5. *Times of India*, 25 October 1940.
6. Ibid.
7. For a fascinating history of the War, see Raghavan, *India's War*.
8. *Times of India*, 24 September 1940. At least three were paid for from proceeds of the Tata collection drive.
9. *Times of India*, 13 December 1941.
10. Lala, *Joy of Achievement*.
11. Piramal, *Business Legends*, p. 471.
12. *Times of India*, 13 December 1941.
13. *Times of India*, 25 October 1940.
14. For war profits, see: Jain, *Indian Economy during the War*, pp. 33–36; Grajdanzev, 'India's Economic Position in 1944', pp. 460–77.
15. Mehta, *Cotton Mills of India*, pp. 193–98.
16. Tripathi, *Dynamics of a Tradition*, pp. 85–100.
17. Singh and Joshi, *Shri Ram*, pp. 45–46.

18. Ibid., p. 52.
19. Jain, *Indian Economy during the War*, p. 38.
20. For the story of the chemical industry, see De Sousa, *History of the Chemical Industry in India*. For a concise contemporary analysis of the impact of the War, see Lokanathan, *India's Post-War Reconstruction*.
21. *Times of India*, 25 October 1940.
22. *Times of India*, 18 December 1940.
23. Wadia and Merchant, *Our Economic Problem*, p. 427.
24. *Economist*, 11 November 1944.
25. Grajdanzev, 'India's Economic Position in 1944', p. 471.
26. Cooper Allen and Bata worked for twenty hours a day, installed new machinery and brought new units into production, but could still only supply standardized boots to the defence services. See Aggarwal, *History of the Supply Department*, p. 176.
27. Jain, *Indian Economy during the War*, p. 46.
28. Ibid., p. 48.
29. *Times of India*, 25 October 1940.
30. Parekh et al., *India in Transition through the Eyes of a Visionary*, p. 1.
31. Ibid.
32. Jain, *Indian Economy during the War*, pp. 29–31.
33. Wadia and Merchant, *Our Economic Problem*, p. 431.
34. Jain, *Indian Economy during the War*, p. 86.
35. *Times of India*, 31 March 1943.
36. Jain, *Indian Economy during the War*, pp. 55–57. Ibid., p. 55.
37. Ibid.
38. Wadia and Merchant, *Our Economic Problem*, pp. 427, 449.

39. Jain, *Indian Economy during the War*, pp. 58–63.
40. Ibid., p. 59.
41. *Times of India*, 16 October 1941.
42. Farley, 'US–India Trade Prospects', pp. 113–14.
43. Lokanathan, *India's Post-War Reconstruction*.
44. Moraes, *Sir Purshottamdas Thakurdas*, pp. 214–17. Also see *Times of India*, 12 June 1940.
45. *Indian Express* (Madras), 5 June 1942. Cited in Birla Papers, Series II, File no. G-11.
46. FICCI, *Correspondence and Relevant Documents 1940–41*.
47. *Capital*, 24 October 1940 and 6 March 1941.
48. *Eastern Economist*, 3 December 1943.
49. Voigt, *India in the Second World War*, pp. 72–73.
50. See Kudaisya, *Life and Times of G.D. Birla*, Chapter 8.
51. Voigt, *India in the Second World War*, p. 108.
52. Ibid.
53. Kudaisya, *Life and Times of G.D. Birla*, Chapter 8.
54. Birla to N.R. Sarkar, 31 January 1943. Birla Papers, Series II, File no. S-4.
55. Report of meeting held at Birla House, New Delhi. Birla Papers, Series II, File no. K-4.
56. *Capital*, 17 June 1943.
57. *Eastern Economist*, 23 June 1944.
58. Venkatsubbiah, *Enterprise and Economic Change*, pp. 43–44.
59. Joshi, *Lala Shri Ram*, p. 187.
60. Ibid.
61. JRD to Sir Jehangir Ghandy, 18 February 1942, in Mambro, *JRD Tata Letters*, pp. 93–94.
62. Lala, *Joy of Achievement*, p. 61.

63. Birla, however, persisted with his plans and, in 1942, finally set up his factory, not in British India but in the princely state of Baroda. See Rao, *B.M. Birla*, pp. 25–26. For the full story of Walchand Hirachand's plans, see Khanolkar, *Walchand Hirachand*, pp. 431–56.
64. FICCI, *Proceedings of the 15th Annual Session, 7–8 March 1942*.
65. *Indian Express* (Madras), 5 June 1942, news clipping. Birla Papers, Series II, File no. G-11.
66. Nehru criticized the government in an article entitled 'Apathy to Indian Motor Industry'. Khanolkar, *Walchand Hirachand*, p. 465.
67. Jain, *Indian Economy during the War*, p. 52.
68. FICCI press communique. Birla Papers, Series II, File no. G-11. Also see Khanolkar, *Walchand Hirachand*, pp. 393–97.
69. Anstey, 'Review of' "Our Economic Problem"', pp. 69–71.
70. Raghavan, *India's War*, pp. 326, 331.
71. *The Economist,* 2 May 1942.

Chapter 2: The Sterling Balance and India's Future

1. Known as 'home charges', this included interest on debt, interest paid to railway companies as annuities, expenses of the secretary of state's office in London, cost of stores for India, and pension and furlough payments to British civil and military officers.
2. Under the Defence Expenditure Plan of February 1940, Britain agreed to pay for the reorganization of the Indian Army, for the costs incurred to maintain British armed

forces in India and for the deployment of Indian troops beyond the subcontinent.

3. The mechanism for payment was the Reserve Bank of India's obligation to buy at '1s 6d' (1 shilling 6 pence) a rupee all sterling offered to it.

4. *Economist,* 6 March 1943.

5. On the sterling issue, see Tomlinson, 'Indo-British Relations in the Post-Colonial Era'; Mukherjee, 'Indo-British Finance', pp. 229–51. For the larger picture, see Schenk, *Britain and the Sterling Area.*

6. Birla to Thakurdas, October 1941. Birla Papers, Series II, File no. T-5: 'Thakurdas, Purshottamdas, Sir'.

7. Birla to Thakurdas, 10 December 1942. Birla Papers, Series II, File no. T-5: 'Thakurdas, Purshottamdas, Sir'.

8. Birla to Thakurdas, 4 August 1942. Birla Papers, Series II, File no. T-5: 'Thakurdas, Purshottamdas, Sir'.

9. Birla to Thakurdas, 4 August 1942. Birla Papers, Important Series II, File no. T-5: 'Thakurdas, Purshottamdas, Sir'.

10. Ibid.

11. Birla to Thakurdas, 26 November 1942. Birla Papers, Series II, File no. T-5: 'Thakurdas, Purshottamdas, Sir'.

12. S.C. Majumdar to Birla, 17 December 1942. Birla Papers, Series II, File no. L-3: 'Lokanathan, P.S., Dr'. Birla to Thakurdas, 26 November 1942. Birla Papers, Series II, File no. T-5: 'Thakurdas, Purshottamdas, Sir'. Birla to Majumdar, 25 March 1943. Birla Papers, Series II, File no. L-3: 'Lokanathan, P.S., Dr'.

13. Birla to Majumdar, 25 March 1943. Birla Papers, Important Series II, File no. L-3: 'Lokanathan, P.S. Dr'.

14. Piramal, *Business Legends*, pp. 385–86.

15. Mehta, *Cotton Mills of India*, p. 217.

16. Mukherjee, *Imperialism, Nationalism*, p. 152.
17. Thakurdas, press statement, 8 June 1944. In Purshottamdas Thakurdas Papers, File no. 324, Part I.
18. *Eastern Economist*, 16 July 1943.
19. *Times of India*, 17 August 1943.
20. For instance, C.D. Deshmukh, deputy governor of the Reserve Bank, was optimistic that the sterling would be available for imports for the expansion of industries, industrial reconstruction and rural development (*Times of India*, 17 August 1943).
21. Mukherjee, *Imperialism, Nationalism*, pp. 148–49.
22. Thakurdas, 'Currency and Exchange', pp. 146–51.
23. *FICCI, Proceedings of Annual Meeting 1943*.
24. Dadabhoy, *Barons of Banking*, p. 232.
25. P.B., 'The Sterling Balances', pp. 353–62.
26. Mukherjee, *Imperialism, Nationalism*, pp. 146–49.
27. Ibid., pp. 148–241.
28. Birla argued that the index number should be fixed from time to time as further accumulation took place, and that all debts be repaid within a certain period of time.
29. Birla, *Inflation or Scarcity*, p. 29.
30. Thakurdas, 'Currency and Exchange', pp. 146–51.
31. Press statement issued by FICCI, 10 October 1942. Cited in Mukherjee, *Imperialism, Nationalism*, p. 108.
32. Birla to Thakurdas, 10 December 1942, Birla Papers, Important Series, File no. T-5.
33. FICCI, *Correspondence and Relevant Documents Relating to Important Questions*, no. F 465|437, dated 11 March 1943.
34. Mukherjee, *Imperialism, Nationalism*, p. 153.
35. War Cabinet, *Conclusions of a Meeting, August 6, 1942*.

36. 'India's Sterling Balances', Bank of England Archive: M5/537, p. 1233.
37. Dadabhoy, *Barons of Banking*, p. 234.
38. Thakurdas, press statement, 8 June 1944. Purshottamdas Thakurdas Papers, File 324, Part I.
39. Birla, *Bombay Chronicle*, 6 June 1944. Cited in Mukherjee, *Imperialism, Nationalism*, p. 144.
40. Vakil, *Falling Rupee*.
41. Jain, *Indian Economy during the War*, p. 80; Vakil, *Falling Rupee*, p. 124. Also see B.R. Shenoy, *Times of India*, 22 January 1943.
42. Dasgupta, 'Preface', in *War and Post-War Inflation in India*.
43. Jain, *Indian Economy during the War*, p. 81.
44. See 'Manifesto by Indian Economists on the Recent Economic Policy of the Government of India', 12 April 1943, in Vakil, *Financial Burden of the War on India*, Appendix I, pp. 134–37.
45. Shah, *How India Pays for the War*, p. 110.
46. See in Kudaisya, *Life and Times of G.D. Birla*, Chapter 8: 'The War Years'.
47. Vakil was probably alluding to Birla when, many years later in 1977, he spoke of the 1943 inflation debate and the 'systematic propaganda by a leading industrialist close to the Congress against my suggestions'. See *Times of India*, 10 August 1977.
48. Birla, *War Finance under a National Government*.
49. Birla, *Inflation or Scarcity*, p. 35.
50. Birla, *Inflation or Scarcity*.
51. Birla to Kasturbhai, 23 April 1944. Birla Papers, Important Series II, File no. K-4: 'Kasturbhai, Lalbhai'.

52. Lokanathan, *India's Post War Reconstruction*, p. 30.
53. Ibid.
54. This box item draws entirely upon Balachandran, *Reserve Bank of India*.

Chapter 3: The Authors of the Plan

1. Sarkar, *Modern India*, p. 394.
2. Birla to JRD Tata, 14 November 1942; JRD Tata to Birla, 25 November 1942. Birla Papers, Important Files, Series II, File no. T-1: 'Tata, JRD'.
3. *The Economist*, 17 June 1944.
4. Moraes, *Sir Purshottamdas Thakurdas*, pp. 164–82.
5. Sen, *Dictionary of National Biography*, vol. IV, pp. 339–40; Moraes, *Sir Purshottamdas Thakurdas*.
6. Sen, *Dictionary of National Biography*, vol. IV, pp. 339–40.
7. Moraes, *Sir Purshottamdas Thakurdas*, pp. 21–23. Also see *Times of India*, 17 July 1919.
8. Gordon, *Businessmen and Politics*, pp. 180–84.
9. Moraes, *Sir Purshottamdas Thakurdas*, p. 213.
10. Gordon, *Businessmen and Politics*, p. 10.
11. Dwijendra Tripathi, 'Congress and Indian Industrialists, 1885–1947', in Tripathi, *Business and Politics in India*, p. 97.
12. Thakurdas to T. Holland, 16 October 1920; Ardeshir Dalal to Thakurdas, 19 October 1920. In Purshottamdas Thakurdas Papers, File no. 24/II.
13. Gordon, *Businessmen and Politics*, pp. 159, 217–22.
14. *Times of India*, 20 May 1936.
15. Thakurdas to Birla, 17 June 1943. Birla Papers, Important Series II, File no. T-6: 'Thakurdas, Purshottamdas, Sir'.

16. Lala, *Joy of Achievement*, p. 19.

17. *Times of India*, 3 March 1939 and 4 May 1939.

18. Tripathi, *Oxford History of Indian Business*, p. 179; *Times of India*, 7 March 1939.

19. Lala, *Joy of Achievement*, p. 49.

20. *Guardian*, 30 November 1993.

21. *Times of India*, 30 November 1993.

22. Lala, *Beyond the Last Blue Mountain*; Lala, *Joy of Achievement*.

23. Markovits, *Indian Business and Nationalist Politics*, p. 76.

24. Tripathi, *Oxford History of Indian Business*, p. 182.

25. See Kudaisya, *Life and Times of G.D. Birla*, pp. 169–71.

26. Ibid., p. 281.

27. See Tripathi, *Dynamics of a Tradition*.

28. Tripathi, 'Congress and Indian Industrialists, 1885–1947', in Tripathi, *Business and Politics in India*, pp. 98–99; Tripathi, *Oxford History of Indian Business*, p. 263.

29. D.A. Low, 'The Forgotten Bania Merchant Communities and the Indian National Congress', in Low, *Indian National Congress*.

30. He possessed only a bare four dhotis, eight shirts and four long coats, all bought just once a year. Piramal, *Business Legends*, pp. 355–56.

31. Tripathi, *Oxford History of Indian Business*, pp. 192–93.

32. Tripathi, *Business and Politics in India*, pp. 104–05.

33. Piramal, *Business Legends*.

34. Markovits, *Indian Business and Nationalist Politics*, p. 112.

35. Spodek, *Ahmedabad*, p. 124.

36. See Singh and Joshi, *Shri Ram*.

37. S. Ambirajan, 'Changing Attitudes towards Business in India', in Tripathi, *Business and Politics in India*. Also see Singh and Joshi, *Shri Ram*, pp. 201–02.

38. Ram, *The DCM Story*, p. 38.
39. Bhupesh Bhandari, 'Remembering Bharat Ram'. *Business Standard*, 9 October 2014, http://www.business-standard. com/article/opinion/bhupesh-bhandari-remembering-bharat-ram-114100901277_1.html.
40. Singh and Joshi, *Shri Ram*, p. 23.
41. On Shroff, see Dalal, *A.D. Shroff*, pp. 12–20.
42. Ibid., pp. 8–9.
43. Gordon, *Businessmen and Politics*, pp. 155–99.
44. *Times of India*, 'Letter to the Editor', 15 July 1930.
45. *Times of India*, 'Letter to the Editor', 15 March 1929.
46. *Times of India*, 25 October 1930.
47. *Times of India*, 'Letter to the Editor', 25 October 1930.
48. Markovits, *Indian Business and Nationalist Politics*, *Times of India*, 29 April 1936, 30 April 1936 and 20 May 1936.
49. Markovits, *Indian Business and Nationalist Politics*, pp. 109–13.
50. *Times of India*, 30 April 1936 and 20 May 1936.
51. J.R.D. Tata, in Shroff, *On Planning and Finance*.
52. A.D. Shroff's letter to the editor, *Times of India*, 20 June 1940.
53. Lala, *Joy of Achievement*, p. 48.
54. Gilbert, *Some South Indian Villages*. Also see review of Gilbert's book by Lokanathan in *The Economic Journal* 47, no. 185 (March 1937): 144–47.
55. Pappu, 'Dr P.S. Lokanathan', p. 293.
56. See Dalal, *A.D. Shroff*.
57. See Kudaisya, *Life and Times of G.D. Birla*, Chapter 6.
58. See FICCI, *Correspondence and Relevant Documents 1942–43*.
59. See Markovits, *Indian Business and Nationalist Politics*, Chapter 6.

60. See letter to the secretary of the viceroy, 4 August 1942, from Birla, Tata, Thakurdas and others. Birla Papers, Series II, File no. G-II.

61. Thakurdas to Birla, 17 June 1943. Birla Papers, Important Series II, File no. T-6: 'Thakurdas, Purshottamdas, Sir'.

62. Letter to the secretary of the viceroy, 4 August 1942, from Birla, Tata, Thakurdas and others. Birla Papers, Series II, File no. G-II.

Chapter 4: The Intellectual Context of the Plan

1. On these debates, see Robbins, *Autobiography of an Economist*. Also see Coase, 'Economics at LSE in the 1930s', pp. 31–34; and Christainsen, 'What Keynes Really Said to Hayek about Planning', pp. 50–53.

2. Robbins, *Autobiography of an Economist*, p. 127.

3. See Coats, 'The Distinctive LSE Ethos'.

4. Hall, *Political Power of Economic Ideas*, p. 6.

5. Ibid., pp. 6–7.

6. On the ideas of Hayek, see McCormick, *Hayek and the Keynesian Avalanche*.

7. Pigou, 'Review of *The Road to Serfdom*', pp. 217–19.

8. Ibid.

9. Pigou, 'Presidential Address', pp. 215–21.

10. Pigou, *Socialism versus Capitalism*.

11. Crowther, 'Must Capitalism and Communism Clash?'

12. Keynes, *General Theory of Employment, Interest and Money*.

13. Hayek, *Road to Serfdom*.

14. On these debates, see Kevin D. Hoover, 'A History of Post-war Monetary Economics and Macroeconomics', in Samuels et al. (eds), *A Companion to the History of Economic Thought*, pp. 411–27.

15. See McCormick, *Hayek and the Keynesian Avalanche*.
16. Hall, *Political Power of Economic Ideas*.
17. McCormick, *Hayek and the Keynesian Avalanche*, p. 185.
18. Dahrendorf, *LSE*, p. 220.
19. Ibid.
20. Skidelsky, *Keynes*, p. 59.
21. See Gordon, *Businessmen and Politics*, pp. 180–85.
22. J.M. Keynes, 'Evidence before Royal Commission on Indian Currency and Finance', in Robinson and Moggridge, *Collected Works of John Maynard Keynes, vol. XIX*, pp. 477–78.
23. Ibid., pp. 496–506.
24. Chandavarkar, *Keynes and India*, pp. 84–85.
25. Toye, *Labour Party and the Planned Economy*, p. 3.
26. Ibid.
27. *New York Times*, 11 April 1978.
28. On the debates, see Zachariah, *Developing India*.
29. Gyanchand, 'The Essentials of Economic Planning for India', in Krishnamurty, *Towards Development Economics*, pp. 173–83.
30. Influenced by Vivekananda and Bankim Chandra, Roy (1887–1954) had joined the Bengal Revolutionary movement as a teenager. Described by Lenin as 'the symbol of revolution in the East', Roy had founded the Communist Party of Mexico in 1919 and the Communist Party of India in 1920.
31. See M.N. Roy, 'Planning and Planning', in Banerjea, *Alphabet of Fascist Economics*, pp. 61–104.
32. For some of these ideas see V.K.R.V. Rao, 'Nehru's Economic Vision', in Dixit et al., *Jawaharlal Nehru Centenary Volume*.
33. On these debates, see Dasgupta, *A History of Indian Economic Thought*, p. 133.

34. Ibid., p. 139.

35. Zachariah, *Developing India*. For Gandhian ideas, see Agarwal, *The Gandhian Plan for Economic Development for India*; Govindu and Malghan, *The Web of Freedom*.

36. On these debates, see Chattopadhyay, 'The Idea of Planning in India'.

37. Gyanchand, 'The Essentials of Economic Planning for India', in Krishnamurty, *Towards Development Economics*, p. 178.

Chapter 5: The Plan Analysed

1. Commercial Printing Press, Bombay, January 1944.

2. Bombay Plan, Part II, p. 27.

3. Bombay Plan, Part I, p. 2.

4. Lokanathan, *India's Post-War Reconstruction*, p. 57.

5. Zachariah, *Developing India*; 'British and Indian Ideas of "Development"'.

6. Masani, *Picture of a Plan*, p. 47.

7. Ibid., p. 42.

8. Ibid., p. 43.

9. Bombay Plan, Part I, p. 4.

10. Bombay Plan, Part II, pp. 5–6. Also Masani, *Picture of a Plan*, p. 42.

11. Masani, *Picture of a Plan*, p. 42.

12. Ibid.

13. Ibid.

14. Ibid., p. 44.

15. Ibid., p. 1.

16. Bombay Plan, Part I, p. 28.

17. Ibid., p. 2.

18. Masani, *Picture of a Plan*, p. 4.

19. Ibid., p. 5.
20. Ibid., p. 6.
21. Lokanathan, 'The Bombay Plan', pp. 680–86.
22. Masani, *Picture of a Plan*, pp. 12–13.
23. See Chapter 3 of Srinivasan, *Eight Lectures on India's Economic Reforms*, for different calculations of the poverty line.
24. Lokanathan, 'The Bombay Plan', pp. 680–86.
25. Ibid.
26. Masani, *Picture of a Plan*, p. 29.
27. Bombay Plan, Part I, p. 4.
28. Ibid., p. 26.
29. Ibid., pp. 26–27.
30. Masani, *Picture of a Plan*, p. 31.
31. Ibid., p. 22.
32. Ibid.
33. Masani, *Picture of a Plan*, pp. 25–26.
34. Bombay Plan, Part I, pp. 30–31.
35. Masani, *Picture of a Plan*, p. 23.
36. Bombay Plan, Part 1, p. 35.
37. G.D. Birla to Horace Alexander, 4 October 1944. Birla Papers, Foreign Correspondence, File no. 3, 1935–46.
38. Ibid.
39. G.D. Birla to Matthai, January 1943. Purshottamdas Thakurdas Papers, File no. 291, 1942—Part I.
40. G.D. Birla to Horace Alexander, 4 October 1944. Birla Papers, Foreign Correspondence, File no. 3, 1935–46.
41. Bombay Plan, Part I, pp. 31–32; letter from G.D. Birla to Horace Alexander, Birla Papers, Foreign Correspondence, File no. 3, 1935–46.
42. Bombay Plan, Part I, pp. 32–33.

43. Bombay Plan, Part II, pp. 20–22.
44. Bombay Plan, Part I, pp. 35–38.
45. Ibid., pp. 46-47.
46. Ibid.
47. Ibid.
48. Masani, *Picture of a Plan*, p. 34.
49. Bombay Plan, Part I, pp. 45–50.
50. Ibid., p. 34.
51. Ibid., pp. 35–36.
52. Ibid., p. 36.
53. Lokanathan, 'The Bombay Plan', pp. 680–86.
54. Bombay Plan, Part I, p. 49.
55. Lokanathan, 'Development Programs in China and India', pp. 84–93.
56. Ibid.
57. Masani, *Picture of a Plan*, p. 40.
58. Bombay Plan, Part II, p. 6.
59. Ibid., p. 10.
60. Masani, *Picture of a Plan*, p. 47.
61. Ibid., pp. 47–49.
62. Bombay Plan, Part II, p. 19.
63. Ibid., p. 20.
64. Masani, *Picture of a Plan*, p. 51.
65. Bombay Plan, Part II, pp. 24–25.
66. Ibid.
67. Ibid.
68. Ibid., p. 26.
69. Ibid.
70. Masani, *Picture of a Plan*, p. 57.
71. Bombay Plan, Part II, p. 31.
72. Ibid., pp. 31–32.
73. Masani, *Picture of a Plan*, pp. 62–63.

74. Bombay Plan, Part II, p. 27.
75. Masani, *Picture of a Plan*, p. 59.
76. Bombay Plan, Part II, p. 28.
77. Ibid., pp. 28–29.
78. Bombay Plan, Part II, p. 31.
79. Ibid., pp. 30–31.

Chapter 6: The Plan and the Public

1. Lokanathan, *India's Post-War Reconstruction*, p. 57.
2. G.D. Birla to J.R.D. Tata, 10 April 1944. Birla Papers, Important Files, Series II, File no. T-1: 'Tata, J.R.D'.
3. G.D. Birla to Devdas Gandhi, 18 January 1944. Birla Papers, Series II, File no. G-5: 'Gandhi, Devdas'.
4. *Times of India*, 18 January 1945.
5. *Times of India*, 14 February 1944, 10 October 1944 and 26 June 1944.
6. *Times of India*, 2 March 1944.
7. An LLB from London University and barrister-at-law from Lincoln's Inn, Masani (1905–98) had been attracted to socialism and Marxist ideas during his stay in London. He later joined the Indian National Congress and was appointed president of the Bombay provincial Congress committee in 1933. A year later, along with Jayaprakash Narayan, he launched the Congress Socialist Party. By 1939, however, disenchanted with the Left, he resigned from the party he helped found and joined the Tatas in 1941 where he worked for sixteen years. In 1945, Masani became a nominated member of the central legislative assembly. He was also a member of the Constituent Assembly. In the 1950s, he became a trenchant critic of the Nehru government. He was

an important founder–member of the Forum of Free
Enterprise set up by A.D. Shroff in 1956, and of the
Swatantra Party in 1960 along with C. Rajagopalachri
and N.G. Ranga. For more details on Masani, see Raju,
Minoo Masani, and Erdman, *Swatantra Party and Indian
Conservatism*.

8. Masani, 'Preface', *Our India*.
9. J.R.D. Tata to G.D. Birla, 8 September 1944. Birla
Papers, Important Files, Series II, File no. T-1: 'Tata,
J.R.D.'.
10. G.D. Birla to J.R.D. Tata, 12 September 1944. Birla
Papers, Important Files, Series II, File no. T-1: 'Tata,
J.R.D.'.
11. J.R.D. Tata to G.D. Birla, 17 November 1945. Birla
Papers, Important Files, Series II, File no. T-1: 'Tata,
J.R.D.'.
12. G.D. Birla to J.R.D. Tata, 24 November 1945. Birla
Papers, Important Files, Series II, File no. T-1: 'Tata,
J.R.D.'.
13. Tata Sons Ltd, *Public Relations Department. Review:
1943–50*, Tata Central Archives, A.D. Shroff Papers:
ICI-ADS-216 (Box 425).
14. *The Times* (London), 23 June 1944.
15. J.R.D. Tata to G.D. Birla, 5 April 1944, and G.D. Birla
to J.R.D. Tata, 10 April 1944. Birla Papers, Important
Files, Series II, File no. T-1: 'Tata, J.R.D.'.
16. *New York Times*, 21 May 1944.
17. *Washington Post*, 6 August 1944; *Observer*, 20 May 1945.
18. *Chicago Daily Tribune*, 14 May 1946.
19. *Times* (London), 31 May 1944.
20. *Observer*, 20 May 1945.
21. *Manchester Guardian*, 27 May 1944 and 5 July 1944.

22. *Times of India*, 29 June 1944.
23. Ibid.
24. *Economist*, 17 June 1944, 8 July 1944.
25. *Times of India*, 21 April 1944.
26. *Times* (London), 31 May 1944.
27. See Bhattacharya and Zachariah, 'A Great Destiny'.
28. *Times of India*, 20 April and 21 April 1944.
29. On the background, see Moon, *Wavell: The Viceroy's Journal*, pp. 66–67.
30. *Times* (London), 1 June 1944.
31. *Times of India*, 2 June 1944.
32. Moon, *Wavell*, pp. 66–67.
33. G.D. Birla to Devdas Gandhi, 13 January 1946. Birla Papers, Series II, File no. G- 5: 'Gandhi, Devdas'.
34. *Times of India*, 25 August 1944.
35. Visvesvaraya, *Planned Economy for India*. Also see Zachariah, *Developing India*.
36. For debates in the Assembly on the Bombay Plan, see *Times of India*, 25 August 1944, 19 October 1944, 18 November 1944 and 21 November 1944.
37. Anstey, 'Review of "A Plan for Economic Development for India"', pp. 555–57.
38. *Times of India*, 5 June 1944.
39. Ibid.
40. Agarwala, A.N., Benares, 1944.
41. J.R.D. Tata to G.D. Birla, 12 August 1944. Birla Papers, Important Files, Series II, File no. T-1: 'Tata, J.R.D.'.
42. Ibid.
43. G.D. Birla to J.R.D. Tata, 15 August 1944. Birla Papers, Important Files, Series II, File no. T-1: 'Tata, J.R.D.'.
44. Agarwal, *Gandhian Plan of Economic Development for India*.

45. Ibid., p. 2: Foreword written by Mahatma Gandhi, 16 October 1944.
46. Banerjea, *Alphabet of Fascist Economics*.
47. Roy, 'Planning and Planning', in Banerjea, *Alphabet of Fascist Economics*.
48. Ibid.
49. Banerjea, *Alphabet of Fascist Economics*.
50. Wadia and Merchant, *The Bombay Plan: A Criticism*.
51. G.D. Birla to J.R.D. Tata, 15 August 1944. Birla Papers, Series II, File no. T-I: 'Tata, J.R.D.'.
52. *Manchester Guardian*, 5 July 1944.
53. See Shenoy, *The Bombay Plan*.
54. Lokanathan, *India's Post-War Reconstruction*, pp. 55–56.
55. *Manchester Guardian*, 6 July 1944.
56. G.D. Birla to Schuster, 2 January 1944. Birla Papers, Foreign Correspondence, File no. S-18, 1935–46.
57. G.D. Birla to H.M. Patel, 16 February 1945. Birla Papers.
58. See 'Report of Visit to the UK and the USA of a Group of Indian Industrialists', Tata Archives, ICI-ADS-215 (Box 425).
59. J.R.D. Tata to Betty Hutheesing, 21 March 194. J.R.D. Tata Papers: JRDT/Misc/5 (Box 354).
60. 'Report of the Visit to the UK and the USA of a Group of Indian Industrialists', Tata Central Archives, ICI-ADS-215 (Box 425).
61. Gandhi's statement to the Press, Mahabaleshwar, 6 May 1945, in *Collected Works of Mahatma Gandhi* vol. 80, p. 80.
62. Copy of G.D. Birla's telegram sent on 7 May 1945 to Gandhi. Tata Central Archives, J.R.D. Tata Papers JRDT/Misc/7 (Box 354).

63. Typed copy of J.R.D. Tata's statement to the Press, 8 May 1945. Tata Central Archives, J.R.D. Tata Papers: JRDT/File 3/7 (Box 354).

64. Gandhi to J.R.D. Tata, 10 May 1945, in *Collected Works of Mahatma Gandhi*, vol. 80, p. 100.

65. Gandhi to G.D. Birla, 8 May 1945, in *Collected Works of Mahatma Gandhi*, vol. 80, p. 94.

66. *Collected Works of Mahatma Gandhi*, vol. 80, p. 94: 'notes'.

67. Gandhi to G.D. Birla, 10 May 1945, in *Collected Works of Mahatma Gandhi*, vol. 80, pp. 102–03.

68. Tata Central Archives, J.R.D Tata Papers, JRDT/File 3/7 (Box 354).

69. See J.R.D. Tata to G.D. Birla, 28 September 1944, in Mambro, *J.R.D. Tata Letters*, pp. 103–04.

70. G.D. Birla to B.M. Birla, 23 May 1945. Birla Papers, Important Series, File no. I-9: 'Interviews with Persons Abroad'. On the response to the mission in the UK, see *Manchester Guardian*, 'Letter to the Editor', 27 May 1944.

71. See J.R.D. Tata to G.D. Birla, 28 September 1944, in Mambro, *J.R.D. Tata Letters*, pp. 103–04.

72. G.D. Birla to B.M. Birla, 10 July 1945. Birla Papers, File no. I-9: 'Interviews with Persons Abroad'.

73. *Times of India*, 18 July and 2 August 1945.

74. *Washington Post*, 6 August 1944.

75. *Times of India*, 5 August 1944.

76. *Times of India*, 'Indian Mission Premature. Mr J.R.D. Tata's View', 2 August 1945.

77. *Manchester Guardian*, 26 September 1945. Also see: A.D. Shroff to Hon. Emanuel Cellar, 13 July 1945. Tata Central Archives. A.D. Shroff Papers, ICI-ADS-213 (Box 425).

78. See 'Report of Visit to the UK and the USA of a Group of Indian Industrialists', A.D. Shroff Papers, ICI-ADS-215 (Box 425), Tata Central Archives.
79. G.D. Birla to B.M. Birla, 2 August 1945. Birla Papers, File no. I-9: 'Interviews with Persons Abroad'.
80. *Times of India*, 2 August 1945.
81. Ibid.
82. G.D. Birla to B.M. Birla, 13 July 1945. Birla Papers, File no. I-9: 'Interviews with Persons Abroad'.

Chapters 7: Afterlife of the Plan

1. Kudaisya, 'A Mighty Adventure', pp. 939–78.
2. V.K.R.V. Rao, 'India's First Five-Year Plan', pp. 3–23.
3. Ibid.
4. Ibid.
5. Ibid.
6. Kulkarni, *Deficit Financing and Economic Development*, p. 187.
7. Singh, 'The Bombay Plan Recalled'. An alumnus of LSE and a member of the ICS, Singh was Nehru's deputy secretary in the interim government. He was perhaps the longest-serving member of the Planning Commission with a deep interest in the rural sector.
8. For a background, see Tan and Kudaisya, *The Aftermath of Partition in South Asia*, and Khan, *The Great Partition*.
9. Vakil, *Economic Consequences of Divided India*, p. 117. Also see Chatterji, *The Spoils of Partition*.
10. Dasgupta, *War and Post-War Inflation in India*, p. 41.
11. Vakil, *Economic Consequences of Divided India*, pp. 30–31.
12. Mody and Matthai, *A Memorandum on the Economic and Financial Aspects of Pakistan*.

13. See *Eastern Economist*, 'Bengal Divided', 25 April 1947 and 27 June 1947.
14. Ibid.
15. Birla, 'Basic Facts Relating to India and Pakistan'.
16. Ibid.
17. Matthai, 'Copy of Dr J.M.'s Manuscript', T-55-T-30. Biodata-DIR-So-John Matthai-06, Tata Central Archives.
18. Rao, 'India's First Five-Year Plan'.
19. Dasgupta, *War and Post-War Inflation in India*.
20. Ibid., p. 38.
21. Singh, 'C.D. Deshmukh and the First Phase in Planning', pp. 294–96.
22. Matthai, 'Copy of Dr J.M.'s Manuscript'.
23. For analyses of the planning experience, see: Balakrishnan, *Economic Growth in India*, 'Visible Hand'; Basu, 'India's Dilemmas', *India's Emerging Economy*, and *The Concise Oxford Companion to Economics in India*; Byres, *The Indian Economy*; Chakrabarty, 'Jawaharlal Nehru and Planning, 1938–1941'; Chakravarty, *Selected Economic Writings*; Das, *India Unbound*, *The Elephant Paradigm* and *India Grows at Night*; Dasgupta, *A History of Indian Economic Thought*; Hansen, *The Process of Planning*; Kamath, 'The Failure of Development Planning in India'; Lewis, *Quiet Crisis in India*; Menon, 'Fancy Calculating Machines', pp. 421–57; Mukherji, *India's Economic Transition*, and *Political Economy of Reforms in India*; Nayyar, *Globalisation and Nationalism* and *India's Mixed Economy*; Nayyar (ed.), *Economics as Ideology and Development*; Roy, 'The British Empire and the Economic Development of India, 1858–1947', pp. 209–36, and *The Economy of South Asia*; Singh, *India's Development*

Experience; Srinivasan, *Indian Economy*; Tomlinson, *The Economy of Modern India*; Ahluwalia and Little, *India's Economic Reforms and Development*;
Streeton and Lipton, *Crisis of Indian Planning*.

24. Venkatsubbiah, *Enterprise and Economic Change*, pp. 84–86, 99–100.

25. Iyengar, 'A Look at the Bombay Plan in the Light of Today'.

26. *Eastern Economist*, 19 August 1966.

27. Birla to UCO Bank on 28 March 1956, as reported in *Eastern Economist*, 30 March 1956.

28. Moraes, *Purshottamdas Thakurdas*, p. 280.

29. FICCI, *Proceedings of 24th session, 31 March–2 April 1951*, p. 16.

30. Speech of Tulsidas Kilachand, in FICCI, *Proceedings of 24th session, 31 March–2 April 1951*, p. 18.

31. For Shroff's views, see Shroff, *On Planning and Finance in India*.

32. Patel, *Glimpses of Indian Economic Policy*.

33. *Times of India*, 25 June 1954.

34. Frankel, *India's Political Economy, 1947–1977*, p. 130.

35. See Patel, *Glimpses of Indian Economic Policy*, p. 63. Also see Chattopadhyay, 'The Idea of Planning in India', p. 357.

36. See Kudaisya, *Life and Times of G.D. Birla*, Chapter 13.

37. Letter from a businessperson to Rajendra Prasad, 13 February 1948, cited in Kochanek, *Business and Politics in India*, p. 167.

38. Kudaisya, *Life and Times of G.D. Birla*, p. 306.

39. Birla to Homi Mody, 18 January 1954; Mody to Birla, 30 January 1954; Mody to Birla, 31 March 1954. In Birla Papers, Series I, File no. M-19: 'Mody, Sir Homi and Russi'. Also see *Eastern Economist*, 30 April 1954.

40. Birla, 'Agenda for Discussion with the Prime Minister', two-page note containing points for discussion suggested by Birla, Kasturbhai and Mody, n.d. Birla Papers, Important Series, File no. 158: Miscellaneous, 1955–56.

41. On FICCI's response to Mahalanobis's ideas, see Frankel, *India's Political Economy*, p. 129.

42. Mody to Birla, 27 December 1955. Birla Papers, Series I, File no. M-19: 'Mody, Sir Homi and Russi'. Birla to G.B. Pant, 20 March 1956. Birla Papers, Foreign Correspondence, File no. 87-P, 1955–56 and Series I, File no. P-10: 'Pant, G.B.'. Birla to Morarji Desai, 27 June 1955. Birla Papers, Series I, File no. D-4: 'Desai, Morarji'.

43. Birla to T.T. Krishnamachari, 20 August 1956. Birla Papers, Foreign Correspondence Series, File no. 82-K, 1955–56.

44. Birla to G.B. Pant, 20 August 1956. Birla Papers, Foreign Correspondence Series, File no. 87-P, 1955–56. Also see: Birla to Nehru, 25 August 1955. Birla Papers, Series I, File no. N-24: 'Nehru, Jawaharlal and Indira Gandhi'.

45. Venkatsubbiah, *Enterprise and Economic Change*.

46. Birla to Mody, 18 January 1954; Mody to Birla, 30 January 1954; Mody to Birla, 31 March 1954. Birla Papers, Series I, File no. M-19: 'Mody, Sir Homi and Russi'.

47. *Times of India*, 14 January 1954.

48. Birla to Mody, 18 January 1954; Mody to Birla, 30 January 1954; Mody to Birla, 31 March 1954. In Birla Papers, Series I, File no. M-19: 'Mody, Sir Homi and Russi'. Also see *Eastern Economist*, 30 April 1954.

49. *Times of India*, 14 January 1954.

50. *Times of India*, 28 April 1954.

51. Piramal, *Bombay Plan and the Frustrations of Sir Ardeshir Dalal*.

52. Kudaisya, 'A Mighty Adventure'.

53. *Times of India*, 3 June 1950.

54. Matthai, 'Copy of Dr J.M.'s Manuscript'.

55. See Nehru to Matthai, 4 June 1950, in Gopal, *Selected Works of Jawaharlal Nehru*, vol. 14 (II), pp. 234–38.

56. See Kudaisya, 'A Mighty Adventure'.

57. Matthai, 'Copy of Dr J.M.'s Manuscript'.

58. Haridasan, *Dr John Matthai*, p. 102.

59. Lala, *Joy of Achievement*, pp. 48–49.

60. *Times of India*, 17 November 1953.

61. Iyengar, 'A Look at the Bombay Plan in the Light of Today'.

62. Erdman, *Swatantra Party and Indian Conservatism*, pp. 66–67.

63. Ibid.

64. Ibid.

65. Venkatsubbiah, *Enterprise and Economic Change*, p. 82; Dalal, *A.D. Shroff*, p. 117.

66. *Times of India*, 13 March 1950.

67. *Economic Weekly*, 26 January 1950.

68. *Times of India*, 31 December 1952.

69. *Times of India*, 2 March 1949.

70. Not just textiles, but other sectors of interest to Shri Ram were suffering too: 'With each passing year,' he lamented, 'I am getting to be more pessimistic about our sugar factories where process is regulated by the state, cess imposed ostensibly for improving cane but in reality used by the state to augment its general revenues. Wages are controlled and not even 10 per cent of the cost of production is in our control.'

71. See Chapter 23 of Moraes, *Purshottamdas Thakurdas*; and Umrigar, 'Crisis in the Cotton Market'.

72. This was viewed as a 'ceiling within a ceiling.' See Moraes, *Purshottamdas Thakurdas*.

73. See *Times of India*, 21 April 1956; Moraes, *Purshottamdas Thakurdas*, p. 281.

74. *Times of India*, 11 June 1954.

75. Moraes, *Purshottamdas Thakurdas*, pp. 270–71.

76. Balachandran, *Reserve Bank of India*, p. 724; also see *Times of India*, 11 January 1957.

77. *Times of India*, 5 July 1952 and 7 July 1952.

78. *Times of India*, 6 June 1954.

79. Lala, *Beyond the Last Blue Mountain*, p. 262.

80. Lala, *Joy of Achievement*, pp. 99, 175.

81. Ibid., p. 99.

82. Ibid.

83. Ibid., p. 5.

84. Ibid., p. 4.

85. Kudaisya, *Life and Times of G.D. Birla*, pp. 313–16.

86. Ibid., Chapter 13.

87. Piramal, *Business Maharajas*, p. 406; Kudaisya, *Life and Times of G.D. Birla*, pp. 289–91.

88. Iyengar, 'A Look at the Bombay Plan in the Light of Today'.

89. On the abolition of the Planning Commission, see Shiv Visvanathan, 'An Ode to the Planning Commission', *The Hindu*, 26 August 2014; and Nikhil Menon, 'Out of Commission', *Indian Express*, 15 July 2014.

90. Iyengar, 'A Look at the Bombay Plan in the Light of Today'.

91. Singh, 'The Bombay Plan Recalled'.

92. Bombay Plan, Part II, pp. 23–24.

93. Ibid.

94. Kudaisya, 'A Mighty Adventure'.

95. See A.K. Dasgupta's 'Introduction' in Choudhury, *The Plans for Economic Development of India*; and 'Deficit Financing and the Second Five-Year Plan', *Economic Weekly*, 2 January 1956.

96. Ibid.

97. Chattopadhyay, 'The Idea of Planning in India', p. 358.

98. Namboodiripad, *Economics and Politics of India's Socialist Pattern*, pp. 116–19.

99. Bombay Plan, Part I, p. 7.

100. Frankel, *India's Political Economy*, p. 85.

101. Singh, 'The Bombay Plan Recalled'.

102. Dasgupta, 'Deficit Financing and the Second Five-Year Plan'. Also see: Choudhury, *The Plans for Economic Development of India*, p. 204.

103. Though deficit planning was accepted, it remained much debated. See Kulkarni, *Deficit Financing and Economic Development*, pp. 230–33, 256. Also see: Dasgupta, 'Deficit Financing and the Second Five-Year Plan'.

BIBLIOGRAPHY

Private Papers

G.D. Birla Papers, New Delhi. In private custody of the
   family
Nehru Memorial Museum and Library
John Matthai Papers
Purshottamdas Thakurdas Papers
Kasturbhai Lalbhai Papers
Tata Central Archives
A.D. Shroff Papers
J.R.D. Tata Papers

FICCI Records Room and Library, New Delhi

Proceedings of the Executive Committee, 1939–47
Correspondence and Relevant Documents for the years
   1939–45
Proceedings of the Annual Meetings, 1940–57

Newspapers and Periodicals

Business Standard, 2014
Capital (Calcutta), 1927–47
Chicago Tribune, 1940–47
Eastern Economist (New Delhi), 1943–69
Economica, 1930–47
Manchester Guardian, 1940–47
New York Times, 1939–54
The Economist, 1939–54
The Guardian, 1942–45
The Observer, 1945–47
The Times (London), 1940–47
The Washington Post, 1940–47
Times of India (New Delhi), 1930–57

The Bombay Plan

Masani, Minoo. *Picture of a Plan*. Bombay: Oxford University Press, 1945.

Purshottamdas Thakurdas, J.R.D. Tata, G.D. Birla, Ardeshir Dalal, Shri Ram, Kasturbhai Lalbhai, A.D. Shroff and John Matthai. *A Brief Memorandum Outlining a Plan of Economic Development for India*, Part I. Bombay: Commercial Printing Press, January 1944.

Purshottamdas Thakurdas, J.R.D Tata, G.D Birla, Shri Ram, Kasturbhai Lalbhai, A.D. Shroff and John

Matthai. *A Brief Memorandum Outlining a Plan of Economic Development for India,* Part II: *Distribution—Role of the State.* Bombay: Commercial Printing Press, December 1944.

Published Collections of Source Material

Chopra, P.N., ed. *Towards Freedom: Documents on the Movement for Independence in India.* New Delhi: Oxford University Press, 1986.

Gandhi, M. *The Collected Works of Mahatma Gandhi.* Ahmedabad, 1958–84.

Gopal, S., ed. *Selected Works of Jawaharlal Nehru.* New Delhi: Jawaharlal Nehru Memorial Fund, 1993.

Gupta, P.S., ed. *Towards Freedom: Documents on the Movement for Independence in India.*

Mambro, A., ed. *J.R.D. Tata Letters.* New Delhi: Mehta Publishing House, 2004.

Mansergh, N., and E.W.R. Lumby, eds. *Constitutional Relations between Britain and India: The Transfer of Power, 1942.* Richmond: H.M. Stationery Office, 1981.

Robinson, Austin, and Donald Moggridge. *Collected Works of John Maynard Keynes.* Cambridge: Cambridge University Press, 2012.

———. *Collected Works of John Maynard Keynes Vol XIX. Activities 1924–9: The Return to Gold and Industrial Policy,* Part II, 1981.

Unpublished Dissertation

Chattopadhyay, Raghabendra. 'The Idea of Planning in India, 1930–1951'. Unpublished PhD thesis, Australian National University, Canberra, 1985.

Secondary Sources

Agarwala, A.N., *A Critique of the Industrialists' Plan*. Benares, 1944.

Agarwal, Shriman Narayan. *The Gandhian Plan for Economic Development for India*. Bombay, 1944.

Aggarwal, S.C. *History of the Supply Department 1939–1946*. New Delhi, 1947.

Ahluwalia, Isher Judge, and I.M.D. Little, eds. *India's Economic Reforms and Development: Essays for Manmohan Singh*. New Delhi: Oxford University Press, 1998.

Anstey, Vera. 'Review of "A Plan for Economic Development for India"'. *International Affairs* 41, no. 4 (October 1945): 555–57.

———. 'Review of "Our Economic Problem" by Wadia and Merchant'. *Economica* (New Series) 13, no. 49 (February 1946).

Balachandran, G. *The Reserve Bank of India, 1951–67*. New Delhi: Oxford University Press, 1998.

Balakrishnan, Pulapre. 'Visible Hand: Public Policy and Economic Growth in the Nehru Era'. Mimeo, November 2000.

———. *Economic Growth in India: History and Prospects*. New Delhi: Oxford University Press, 2010.

Bandyopadhyay, Sekhar, ed. *Decolonization and the Politics of Transition in South Asia.* New Delhi: Orient Blackswan, 2014.

Banerjea, B.N. *Alphabet of Fascist Economics: A Critique of the Bombay Plan of Economic Development of India.* Calcutta: Renaissance Publishers, 1944.

Basu, Kaushik. 'India's Dilemmas: The Political Economy of Policy Making in a Globalized World'. *Economic and Political Weekly* 43, no. 5 (February 2008): 53–62.

———. ed. *India's Emerging Economy: Performance and Prospects in the 1990s and Beyond.* Massachusetts: MIT Press, 2004.

———. ed. *The Concise Oxford Companion to Economics in India.* New Delhi: Oxford University Press, 2010.

Bhattacharya, Sanjoy, and Benjamin Zachariah. '"A Great Destiny": The British Colonial State and the Advertisement of Post-War Reconstruction in India, 1942–1945'. *South Asia Research* 19, no. 17 (1999).

Birla G.D. *Inflation or Scarcity?* New Delhi, 1943.

———. *War Finance under a National Government.* n.p., 1943.

———. 'Basic Facts Relating to India and Pakistan'. *Eastern Economist*, Pamphlet no. 5. New Delhi, 1947.

Byres, Terence, ed. *The Indian Economy: Major Debates since Independence.* New Delhi: Oxford University Press, 1998.

Chakrabarty, Bidyut. 'Jawaharlal Nehru and Planning, 1938–1941: India at the Crossroads'. *Modern Asian Studies* 26, no. 2 (1992): 275–87.

Chakravarty, Sukhomoy. *Selected Economic Writings*. New Delhi: Oxford University Press, 1993.

Chandra, Bipan. 'Jawaharlal Nehru and the Capitalist Class'. *Economic and Political Weekly* X, nos 33–35, Special issue, August 1975.

Chandra, Bipan, and Mridula Mukherjee. *India's Struggle for Independence*. New Delhi: Palgrave Macmillan, 1989.

Chandavarkar, Anand. *Keynes and India: A Study in Economics and Biography*. London: Palgrave Macmillan, 1989.

Chatterjee, Partha. *The Nation and Its Fragments: Colonial and Post-Colonial Histories*. Princeton: Princeton University Press, 1999.

Chatterji, Joya. *The Spoils of Partition: Bengal and India, 1947–1967*. Cambridge, 2007.

Chattopadhyay, Raghabendra. 'Attitude of Indian Business towards Economic Planning, 1930–1956'. Published as mimeo online. Paper presented at the IIM Ahmedabad seminar on 'Business and Politics in India: A Historical Perspective', 29–31 March 1989.

Chenoy, Kamal A. *The Rise of Big Business in India*. New Delhi: Aakar Books, 2015.

Chibber, Vivek. *Locked in Place: State-Building and Late Industrialization in India*. Princeton: Princeton University Press, 2003.

Christainsen, Gregory B. 'What Keynes Really Said to Hayek about Planning'. *Challenge*, July–August 1993.

Choudhury, Radharani. *The Plans for Economic Development of India*. Calcutta, 1959.

Coase, R.H. 'Economics at LSE in the 1930s: A Personal View'. *Atlantic Economic Journal* 31 (1982).

Coats, A.W. 'The Distinctive LSE Ethos in the Interwar Years'. *Atlantic Economic Journal* 10, no. 1 (March 1982).

Crowther, Geoffrey. 'Must Capitalism and Communism Clash?' *New York Times*, 6 August 1944.

Dadabhoy, Bakhtiar K. *Barons of Banking: Glimpses of Indian Banking History.* (Noida: Random House India, 2013).

Dalal, Sucheta. *A.D. Shroff: Titan of Finance and Free Enterprise.* New Delhi: Penguin Books, 2000.

Dahrendorf, Ralf. *LSE: A History of the London School of Economics and Political Science, 1895–1995.* New York: Oxford University Press, 1995.

Das, Gurcharan. *India Grows at Night: A Liberal Case for a Strong State.* New Delhi: Penguin Books India, 2012.

———. *India Unbound: From Independence to the Global Information Age.* New Delhi: Penguin Books India, 2002.

———. *The Elephant Paradigm: India Wrestles with Change.* New Delhi: Penguin Books India, 2002.

Dasgupta, A.K. 'Deficit Financing and the Second Five-Year Plan'. *Economic Weekly* 8, nos 3, 4, 5 (January 1956).

———. *War and Post-War Inflation in India.* Calcutta, 1950.

———. *A History of Indian Economic Thought.* London: Routledge, 1993.

De Sousa, J.P. *History of the Chemical Industry in India.* Bombay, 1961.

Dixit, Sheila, K. Natwar Singh, eds. *Jawaharlal Nehru Centenary Volume.* New Delhi, 1989.

Erdman, Howard L. *The Swatantra Party and Indian Conservatism.* Cambridge: Cambridge University Press 1967.

Farley, Miriam S. 'US–India Trade Prospects'. *Far Eastern Survey* 12, no. 11 (1943).

Federation of British Industries. *Reconstruction: A Report of the Federation of British Industries.* London, 1942.

FICCI. *Correspondence and Relevant Documents Relating to Important Questions Dealt with by the Federation during the Year 1940–41.* New Delhi: FICCI, 1941.

Frankel, Francine. *India's Political Economy, 1947–1977: The Gradual Revolution.* Princeton: Princeton University Press, 1978.

Gilbert, Slater. *Some South Indian Villages.* London: Wentworth Press, 1918.

Gordon, A.D.D. *Businessmen and Politics: Rising Nationalism and a Modernizing Economy in Bombay, 1918–1933.* New Delhi: Manohar Publishers, 1978.

Grajdanzev, Andrew J. 'India's Economic Position in 1944'. *Pacific Affairs* 17, no. 4 (December 1944): 460–77.

Govindu, Venu Madhav, and Deepak Malghan. *The Web of Freedom: J.C. Kumarappa and Gandhi's Struggle for Economic Justice.* New Delhi: Oxford University Press, 2016.

Guha, Ram. *India after Gandhi: The History of the World's Largest Democracy.* New York: HarperCollins, 2007.

Hall, Peter A., ed. *The Political Power of Economic Ideas: Keynesianism across Nations.* Princeton: Princeton University Press, 1989.

Hansen, A.H. *The Process of Planning: A Study of India's Five Year Plans, 1950–1964.* London: Oxford University Press, 1966.

Haridasan, V. *Dr John Matthai 1886–1959: A Biography.* Kerala: University of Calicut, 1986.

Hayek, Friedrich von. *The Road to Serfdom.* Chicago: University of Chicago Press, 1944.

Iyengar, H.V.R. 'A Look at the Bombay Plan in the Light of Today'. *Advanced Research in Economic and Management Sciences* 11 (April 2013).

Jain, L.C. *Indian Economy during the War.* Lahore, 1944.

Joshi, Arun. *Lala Shri Ram: A Study in Entrepreneurship and Industrial Management.* New Delhi: Sangam Books, 1979.

Kamath, Shyam J. 'The Failure of Development Planning in India'. In *The Collapse of Development Planning,* edited by Peter J. Boeke. New York: NYU Press, 1994.

Keynes, J.M. *The General Theory of Employment, Interest and Money.* London: Palgrave Macmillan, 1936.

Khan, Yasmin. *The Great Partition: The Making of India and Pakistan.* Yale: Yale University Press, 2007.

Khanolkar, G.D. *Walchand Hirachand.* Bombay, 1969.

Khilnani, Sunil. *The Idea of India.* London: Penguin Books, 1997.

Kochanek, Stanley. *Business and Politics in India.* Berkeley: University of California Press, 1974.

Krishnamurty, J., ed. *Towards Development Economics.* New Delhi: Oxford University Press, 2009.

Kudaisya, Gyanesh. *A Republic in the Making: India in the 1950s*. New Delhi: Oxford University Press, 2017.

Kudaisya, Medha. *The Life and Times of G.D. Birla*. New Delhi: Oxford University Press, 2003.

———. '"A Mighty Adventure": Institutionalizing the Idea of Planning in Post-Colonial India, 1947–60'. *Modern Asian Studies* 43, no. 4 (2009): 939–78.

Kulkarni, R.G. *Deficit Financing and Economic Development with Special Reference to Indian Economic Development*. Bombay: Asia Publishing House, 1966.

Lala, R.M. *Beyond the Last Blue Mountain: A Life of J.R.D. Tata*. New Delhi: Penguin Random House India, 2017.

———. *The Joy of Achievement: Conversations with J.R.D. Tata*. New Delhi: Penguin, 1995.

Lever Brothers and Unilever Limited. *The Problem of Unemployment*. London, 1943.

Lewis, John P. *Quiet Crisis in India: Economic Development and American Policy*. Westport: Greenwood Press, 1967.

Lockwood, David. *The Indian Bourgeoisie: A Political History of the Indian Capitalist Class in the Early Twentieth Century*. New York: I.B. Tauris, 2012.

———. 'Was the Bombay Plan a Capitalist Plot?' *Studies in History* 28, no. 1 (2012): 99–116.

Lokanathan, P.S. 'Development Programs in China and India'. *Pacific Affairs* 18, no. 1 (March 1945).

———. *India's Post-War Reconstruction and Its International Aspects*. New Delhi, 1946.

———. 'The Bombay Plan'. *Foreign Affairs* 23, no. 4 (July 1945).

————. 'Seventy-Second Birthday Commemoration Volume'. *Economic Development Issues and Policies* (Bombay, 1966).

Low, D.A., ed. *The Indian National Congress: Centenary Hindsights.* New Delhi: Oxford University Press, 1988.

Markovits, Claude. *Indian Business and Nationalist Politics 1931–39: The Indigenous Capitalist Class and the Rise of the Congress Party.* Cambridge, 1985.

Masani, Minoo. *Our India.* London: Oxford University Press, 1940.

McCormick, B.J. *Hayek and the Keynesian Avalanche.* New York: Palgrave Macmillan, 1992.

Mehta, S.D. *The Cotton Mills of India, 1854–1954.* Bombay: Textile Association of India, 1954.

Menon, Nikhil. 'Fancy Calculating Machines: Computers and Planning in Independent India'. *Modern Asian Studies* 52, no. 2 (March 2018): 421–57.

Mody, H.M., and J. Matthai. *A Memorandum on the Economic and Financial Aspects of Pakistan.* Bombay, 1945.

Moon, Penderal, ed. *Wavell: The Viceroy's Journal.* London: Oxford University Press, 1973.

Moraes, Frank. *Sir Purshottamdas Thakurdas.* Bombay: Asia Publishing House, 1957.

Mukerjee, Madhushree. *Churchill's Secret War: The British Empire and the Ravaging of India during World War II.* New York: Basic Books, 2010.

Mukherjee, Aditya. 'Indo-British Finance: The Controversy over India's Sterling Balances, 1939–1947'. *Studies in History* 6, no. 2 (1990): 229–51.

————. *Imperialism, Nationalism and the Making of the Indian Capitalist Class, 1920–1947*. New Delhi: Sage Publications, 2002.

Mukherjee, Janam. *Hungry Bengal: War, Famine and the End of Empire*. New York: Oxford University Press, 2015.

Mukherji, Rahul. *India's Economic Transition: The Politics of Reforms*. New Delhi: Oxford University Press, 2007.

————. *Political Economy of Reforms in India*. New Delhi: Oxford University Press, 2014.

Namboodiripad, E.M.S. *Economics and Politics of India's Socialist Pattern*. New Delhi: People's Publishing House, 1966.

Nayyar, Baldev Raj. *India's Mixed Economy: The Role of Ideology and Interest in Development*. Bombay: Popular Prakashan, 1989.

————. *Globalisation and Nationalism: The Changing Balance in India's Economic Policy, 1950–2000*. New Delhi: Sage Publications, 2001.

Nayyar, Deepak, ed. *Economics as Ideology and Development: Essays in Honour of Ashok Mitra*. London: Routledge, 1998.

Pappu, V. 'Dr P.S. Lokanathan'. In *Economic Development: Issues and Policies*, Dr P.S. Lokanathan's seventy-second birthday commemoration volume. Bombay, 1966.

P.B. 'The Sterling Balances: Britain's Debt to the Sterling Area Countries'. *World Today* 2, no. 8 (1946): 353–62.

Paranjape, H.K. *Jawaharlal Nehru and the Planning Commission*. New Delhi: Indian Institute of Public Administration, 1964.

Parekh, H.T., HDFC, and ICICI. *India in Transition through the Eyes of a Visionary, 1940s to 1990s: The Writings of H.T. Parekh: A Tribute by HDFC and ICICI, vol. 1.* Bombay, 1995.

Patel, I.G. *Glimpses of Indian Economic Policy: An Insider's View.* New Delhi: Oxford University Press, 2002.

Pigou, A.C. *Socialism versus Capitalism.* New York: Macmillan, 1937.

————. 'Presidential Address'. *The Economic Journal* 39, no. 194 (1939).

————. 'Review of *The Road to Serfdom*'. *The Economic Journal* 54, no. 214 (1944).

Piramal, Gita. *Business Maharajas.* New Delhi: Penguin Books India, 1996.

————. *Business Legends.* New Delhi, Penguin Books India, 1998.

————. *The Bombay Plan and the Frustrations of Sir Ardeshir Dalal.* Mimeo.

Prakash, Gyan. *Another Reason: Science and the Imagination of Modern India.* Princeton: Princeton University Press, 1999.

Raghavan, Srinath. *India's War: The Making of Modern South Asia 1939–1945.* Gurgaon: Penguin Random House India, 2016.

Raju, S.V. *Minoo Masani.* New Delhi, 2007.

Ram, Vinay Bharat. *From the Brink of Bankruptcy: The DCM Story: The Story of the Growth and Struggle for Survival of a Corporation Born in the Nineteenth Century.* New Delhi: Penguin Books India, 2011.

Rao, Chentsal. *B.M. Birla: His Deeds and Dreams.* New Delhi, 1983.

Rao, V.K.R.V. 'India's First Five-Year Plan: A Descriptive Analysis.' *Pacific Affairs* 25, no. 1 (March 1952): 3–23.

Robbins, Lionel. *Autobiography of an Economist.* London: Palgrave Macmillan, 1971.

Roy, Tirthankar. 'The British Empire and the Economic Development of India, 1858–1947'. *Journal of Iberian and Latin American Economic History* 34, no. 2 (November 2015): 209–36.

———. *The Economy of South Asia: From 1950 to the Present.* New York City: Springer International Publishing, 2017.

Samuels, Warren J., Jeff E. Biddle and John B. Davis, eds. *A Companion to the History of Economic Thought.* New Jersey: Wiley-Blackwell, 2006.

Sanyal, Amal. 'The Curious Case of the Bombay Plan'. *Contemporary Issues and Ideas in Social Sciences* 6, no. 1 (June 2010). Retrieved from nzsac.files.wordpress.com/2012/05/bombayplanfornzsac.pdf.

Sarkar, Sumit. *Modern India.* New Delhi: Macmillan, 1983.

Sen, S.P., ed. *Dictionary of National Biography.* Calcutta, 1974.

Schenk, Catherine R. *Britain and the Sterling Area: From Devaluation to Convertibility in the 1950s.* London: Routledge, 1994.

Schumacher, E.F. 'Bombay Plan: Monetary Theory False'. *Observer*, May 1945.

Shah, K.T. *How India Pays for the War.* Bombay, 1943.

Shenoy, B.R. *The Bombay Plan. A Review of Its Financial Provisions.* Bombay, 1944.

———. *Indian Planning and Economic Development.* Bombay: Asia Publishing House, 1963.

Shroff, A.D. *On Planning and Finance in India.* Bombay: Lalvani Publishing House, 1966.

Singh, Khushwant, and Arun Joshi. *Shri Ram: A Biography.* Mumbai: Asia Publishing House, 1969

Singh, Tarlok. 'The Bombay Plan Recalled'. *Eastern Economist* XL, no. 22, 7 June 1963.

———. *India's Development Experience.* London: Macmillan, 1974.

———. 'C. D. Deshmukh and the First Phase in Planning'. *India International Centre Quarterly* 22, no. 4 (1995).

Skidelsky, Robert. *Keynes: A Very Short Introduction.* Oxford: Oxford University Press, 2010.

Spodek, Howard. *Ahmedabad: Shock City of Twentieth-Century India.* Bloomington: Indiana University Press, 2011.

Srinivasan, T.N. *Eight Lectures on India's Economic Reforms.* New Delhi: Oxford University Press, 2000.

———. *Indian Economy: Current Problems and Future Prospects.* Stanford University, 2003.

Streeton, Paul, and Michael Lipton, eds. *The Crisis of Indian Planning: Economic Planning in the 1960s.* London: Oxford University Press, 1968.

Tan, Tai Yong, and Gyanesh Kudaisya. *The Aftermath of Partition in South Asia.* New Delhi: Psychology Press, 2000.

Thakurdas, Purshottamdas. 'Currency and Exchange'. *India Speaking. The Annals of the American Academy of Political and Social Science* 233 (1944).

Tomlinson, B.R. 'Indo-British Relations in the Post-Colonial Era: The Sterling Balances Negotiations, 1947–49'. *Journal of Imperial and Commonwealth History* 13, no. 3 (1985).

———. *The Economy of Modern India, 1860–1970.* Cambridge: Cambridge University Press, 1993.

Toye, Richard. *The Labour Party and the Planned Economy, 1931–1951.* Suffolk: Royal Historical Society, 2003.

Tripathi, Dwijendra. *The Dynamics of a Tradition: Kasturbhai Lalbhai and His Entrepreneurship.* New Delhi: Manohar Publications, 1981.

———. ed. *Business and Politics in India: A Historical Perspective.* New Delhi: Manohar Publications, 1991.

———. *The Oxford History of Indian Business.* New Delhi: Oxford University Press, 2004.

Umrigar, K.D. 'Crisis in the Cotton Market'. *Economic and Political Weekly,* 19 May 1956.

Vakil, C.N. *Financial Burden of the War on India.* Bombay, 1943.

———. *The Falling Rupee.* Bombay, 1943.

———. *Economic Consequences of Divided India: A Study of the Economy of India and Pakistan.* Bombay, 1950.

Venkatsubbiah, H. *Enterprise and Economic Change: 50 Years of FICCI.* New Delhi: Vikas Publishing House, 1977.

Visvesvaraya, M. *Planned Economy for India.* Bangalore, 1936.

Voigt, J.H. *India in the Second World War*. New Delhi: Arnold-Heinemann, 1987.

Wadia, P.A., and K.T. Merchant. *The Bombay Plan: A Criticism*. Bombay, 1945.

———. *Our Economic Problem*. Bombay, 1957.

War Cabinet, *Conclusions of a Meeting of the War Cabinet held at 10 Downing Street, S-W-1, on Thursday, August 6, 1942, at 5 p.m*, Secret, Copy no. W.M, (42) 105 (52), UK National Archives. Retrieved from http://filestore.nationalarchives.gov.uk/pdfs/large/cab-65-27.pdf.

Whitham, Charles. *Post-War Business Planners in the United States, 1939–1949: The Rise of the Corporate Moderates*. New York: Bloomsbury, 2016.

Zachariah, B. 'British and Indian Ideas of "Development": Decoding Political Conventions in the Late Colonial State'. *Itinerario* 23 , issue 3–4 (November 1999): pp. 162–209.

———. *Developing India: An Intellectual and Social History*. New Delhi: Oxford University Press, 2005.

———. 'India: The Road to the First Five-Year Plan'. In *Decolonization and the Politics of Transition in South Asia*, edited by Bandyopadhyay Sekhar. New Delhi: Orient Blackswan, 2014